Deep Play – Exploring the Use of Depth in Psychotherapy with Children

by the same author

A Manual of Dynamic Play Therapy
Helping Things Fall Apart, the Paradox of Play
Dennis McCarthy
Foreword by Dr David Crenshaw
ISBN 978 1 84905 879 7
eISBN 978 1 85700 644 8

Speaking about the Unspeakable
Non-Verbal Methods and Experiences
in Therapy with Children
Edited by Dennis McCarthy
Foreword by Priscilla Rodgers
ISBN 978 1 84310 879 5
eISBN 978 1 84642 796 1

"If You Turned into a Monster"
Transformation through Play:
A Body-Centred Approach to Play Therapy
Dennis McCarthy
Foreword by Richmond Greene
ISBN 978 1 84310 529 9
eISBN 978 1 84642 628 5

of related interest

Healthy Attachments and Neuro-Dramatic-Play
Sue Jennings
Foreword by Dennis McCarthy
ISBN 978 1 84905 014 2
eISBN 978 0 85700 404 8

Play and Art in Child Psychotherapy
An Expressive Arts Therapy Approach
Ellen G. Levine
ISBN 978 1 84905 504 8
eISBN 978 0 85700 919 7

Deep Play

*Exploring the Use of Depth in
Psychotherapy with Children*

EDITED BY DENNIS MCCARTHY

FOREWORD BY SHAUN MCNIFF

Jessica Kingsley *Publishers*
London and Philadelphia

The poem "My Life Was The Size of My Life" on page 165 by Jane Hirshfield (2014); forthcoming in *The Beauty* (Newcastle: Bloodaxe Books, 2015), is reproduced with kind permission of the author. The poem "For the Children" by Gary Snyder on page 182 is reproduced from *Turtle Island* (New York: New Directions Press, 1974) with kind permission of the author.

First published in 2015
by Jessica Kingsley Publishers
73 Collier Street
London N1 9BE, UK
and
400 Market Street, Suite 400
Philadelphia, PA 19106, USA

www.jkp.com

Copyright © Jessica Kingsley Publishers 2015
Foreword copyright © Shaun McNiff 2015
Index by Emma McCarthy
Front cover image: "Healing Deep Wounds" by Dennis McCarthy

Library of Congress Cataloging in Publication Data
A CIP catalog record for this book is available from the Library of Congress

British Library Cataloguing in Publication Data
A CIP catalogue record for this book is available from the British Library

ISBN 978 1 84905 777 6
eISBN 978 1 78450 104 4

Printed and bound in the United States

For Sherry, who has helped me navigate the depths…

"Childhood" by Joan Monastero

Disclaimer

All the names in the cases mentioned in this text have been changed
as has any information that would render them easily recognizable.
The significant details of the child's play has not been altered.
However, many children and families enter treatment with similar
presenting problems and situations.

Contents

Foreword by Shaun McNiff   9

Introduction   15
Dennis McCarthy

Chapter One   A Deep Story of Deep Play: How the Play, Trance and Séance of the Senoi Temiar People Can Help us Understand Greater Playfulness   23
Dr. Sue Jennings

Chapter Two   Journeying Within: Using Tunnel and Cave Imagery to Access the Inner Imaginative World   37
Timothy Rodier

Chapter Three   The Keys to the World: Revolution and Epiphany in Deep Sand   53
Julie Lyon Rose

Chapter Four   Behold the Treasure and the Swamp! Digging, Delving, Poking, Pounding, and Getting to the Bottom of Things   59
Michelle Rhodes

Chapter Five   Subcutaneous, Subcortical, Subconscious and Subterranean: The Most Toxic Boy in the World's Search for Mum   81
Tim Woodhouse

Chapter Six   Out of the Box and Into the Wild   99
Therese Bimka

Chapter Seven   Deep Sand: Body-centered, Imaginative Play   121
Dennis McCarthy

Chapter Eight   Emergence: A Tale of Two Boys   143
Neal Brodsky

Chapter Nine   Musings about Improving and Deepening
Connections in Families   165
Alan Spivack

Chapter Ten   A Case for In-depth, Long-term Therapy   173
Rob Greene

Epilogue   181
Dennis McCarthy

CONTRIBUTORS   183
SUBJECT INDEX   187
AUTHOR INDEX   190

Foreword

The renewal of free and imaginative play as a way of knowing and transformation is nothing less than urgent if psychotherapy is to keep its depth. The language and thought of practice emphasizing technical and often standardized protocols has moved far afield of soul-work and perhaps no word is more outside the current mindset than "play."

Where this collection of essays concentrates on play as a medium in therapy with children, applications of the ideas and methods expand to all of life, all of therapeutic practice with every age group, and also to research. All of us can return to the source of play in childhood to renew contact with the sensorimotor intelligence, the creative energy that needs to run again through us and our work.

As Dennis McCarthy says, "the good news is that play is still the primary language of children." I think that childhood is keeping the intelligence of imagination alive and intact for all humans. As much as we and our institutions veer away from the creative source into an over-reliance on linear thinking and controls, our successive generations of children preserve the genius.

Those of us who stay close to children witness the wonder and curiosity that is the wellspring of creative imagination in all phases of life. We can return and renew the intelligence of imagination and its languages of creative expression to access ways of knowing simply inaccessible to discursive language, as important as it is in helping us reflect upon, appreciate, and try to communicate what happens spontaneously and unexpectedly through the creative space of play.

The way back to play for older people may take time and discipline, as Picasso said about his lifetime effort "to paint like a child." But it is possible and universally accessible if we are willing to practice and understand the blocks, attitudes, and psychological paradigms that keep it at bay.

When asked how to begin, I say just move and try not to think about what you are going to do before you do it. Let it emerge from your actions. The process is totally reliable if you are able to stay with it. Play and experiment with the materials, move with the paint, the sand, the body, and the space.

Words like return, going back, penetrating, and retrieving what has vanished as in the worldwide indigenous image of illness as "lost soul," imply for many that the restoration of imagination requires going somewhere else, finding something hidden and buried, and digging down after something that is not here. These metaphors are part of the history of depth psychology and its underworlds, alienations, and recovery practices that I admire, but I perversely prefer to imagine depth as what is present and unappreciated in the face of experience – the depth of each gesture that a person makes.

Depth is on the surface of experience unseen; deep down is here now, the only place I can be at this moment, and it is the young children who keep reinforcing this truth. Locating depth somewhere other than now for me feels like a Sisyphean task, an avoidance of the opportunities of the ever-moving moment and the appreciation of its infinite variations and qualities evoked in these pages by the feel of sand and water; the hands and body pushing and pulling, tearing and building; the sounds of the dragons roaring or whispering; the play playing, the sand sanding, the drum drumming, and the magnificent frenzies and pauses of play, the energy and feel of the action that reverberates from player to witness, and how all of this is so much larger than any words or concepts that can only respond to the forces and dynamism of the currents of expression described so well in many of the vignettes of children playing and moving from one thing to another in an overall environment where the creative energy is inside and out, permeating everything and never reduced to one thing.

All we can do is do our best, to be present with it, let it act upon us, and take us where we need to go. Like C.G. Jung's purposeful psyche and self-healing systems mentioned in the chapters of this book, I have found that when creative energy is allowed to circulate freely like the ch'i of Asia, it finds its way to areas of need. There is an intelligence in the process that transcends linear thought and controls.

As I read the authors' free-form descriptions of play sessions, they brought me right back to my early work with young children and the feel of the whole process that I likened to a drama involving all of the senses and all of the arts; the shifts from painting with the whole body standing before an easel and making accompanying sounds, to telling stories about the action, and writing words, and then interpreting it all with more movement in space and me sitting at their level as a quiet witness marveling at how it was all unfolding effortlessly because they were in it, and it was in them, and they took me in too. As the authors say, words "fail" to reduce this complex of action to a single thing, label, concept, or meaning. But they can help us imagine it more insightfully, remember the feeling, and respond to it, especially when we use them creatively. Beginners and experienced therapists will appreciate how this book, from start to finish, gives inspiration and guidance, examples and testimony, convincing evidence that imaginal processes and play-places can exist in our everyday lives, and that they heal.

One of my causes within the arts and therapy disciplines, in many ways inseparable from play therapy when working with young children, is to encourage them to present more direct evidence of what happens – to trust that it will speak for itself, act upon people, and convince them of its effects (McNiff, 2014). As an advocate of artistic inquiry as a way of knowing, I am concerned about the way professions based in creative expression do not show and publish accounts of what they do in ways that look, feel, and sound like it. We have not heard James Hillman's call to speak with a language that psyche understands (1978).

I applaud Dennis McCarthy and his team of contributors for modeling ways of speaking about the work and presenting it, that reverberate with its bodily and energetic grounding together with the creative flights characterizing an immersion in play where the medium and the environment it creates are arguably the most potent healers. I am also impressed with the discussion of what the physical materials of expression do in relation to therapeutic outcomes, something that I have been urging the arts therapy community to explore in more depth. What are the distinct effects and medicines of the substances used – the clay, water, paint, colors, and so forth… how can we use them better? The descriptions in the book about the differences between deep and shallow sand, wet and dry, large and smaller sandboxes, model this perfectly.

The qualities of materials have corresponding influences on the person and the play experience. With the arts in therapy we can be more aware of the material and sensory experiences that are the defining and unique features of what we do…we need to get our hands, bodies, and other senses into the act, feel it, know it better and then talk about it in ways that are consistent with it, rather than trying vainly to translate, explain, and justify it all with paradigms unrelated to what happens in the creative space.

Many of the authors in this volume reinforce how depth is experienced through immersion in the moment, full engagement and presence, and fascination with small things. They also affirm how therapists and leaders support the realization of these states through the creation of a safe space that allows participants to relax their guard, takes risks, let go, and play seriously and with complete concentration. These observations are in keeping with Hans-George Gadamer's point that "seriousness in playing is necessary to make the play wholly play" and that play "fulfills its purpose only if" we lose ourselves in it (1994, p.102). Like the psyche, play is not exclusively subjective and self-immersed. It is objective too, and it shapes the experience of those who do it. It is deep when we are totally involved, when it plays us as Gadamer, who tried to liberate play from "mere" subjectivity, might say. In keeping with Jung's belief in the self-regulating functions that enable the psyche to adjust itself like the body, the authors describe how play is a medium of healing where therapists witness, hold, and help create the safety necessary for the process to unfold as naturally as possible.

In my experience, the depth of the work is reliably accessed by having the freedom and support to engage resistances, fears, and difficult feelings as sources of expression. I call this creating with the shadow – the artistic process in this way corresponds to the dynamics of healing by transforming afflictions into affirmations of life. They are not something to be fixed, eliminated, or cleaned-up. They are to be engaged, and as demonstrated here "played," so they may transform and heal themselves (McNiff, 2015). I feel a close kinship with Dennis McCarthy's history of engaging monsters, unspeakable things, wounds, and the pain of life as openings to creative expression and change. As he says again here, "aggression is a life force" that we learn how to respect and use in positive ways.

Deep Play shows how the so-called bad things may not be so bad if we can change our attitudes and be more artful and playful in relating to them. The deepest and most complete love of the psyche is embracing, holding, and expressing the whole of it.

Shaun McNiff

References

Gadamer, H.-G. (1994). *Truth and Method,* 2nd revised edition (J. Weinsheimer and D. G. Marshall, Trans.). New York, NY: Continuum.

Hillman, J. (1978). *The Myth of Analysis: Three Essays in Archetypal Psychology.* New York, NY: Harper and Row.

McNiff, S. (2014). "Art speaking for itself: Evidence that inspires and convinces." *Journal of Applied Arts & Health,* 5 (2), 255–262.

McNiff, S. (2015). *Imagination in Action: Secrets for unleashing Creative Expression.* Boston, MA and London, UK: Shambhala Publications

Introduction

Dennis McCarthy

In all the old tales, the great stories that still endure, the hero or heroine must go down in order to go up. There is no other way. Jonah is swallowed by the whale and sits deep in its belly in order to be free. Odysseus goes down to the land of the dead and then to the bottom of a whirlpool in order to go home. Bilbo finds "the ring" deep in an underground cavern in Tolkien's *The Hobbit* in order to save his world, although he doesn't know it at the time. Persephone sits in the underworld with Hades and eats the pomegranate seeds so that there may be renewal, the cycle of the seasons. She loses her innocence but is given her name. In other words, she becomes her true self. There is no way forward in this life unless we go down into the depths. To avoid them is to avoid life. Some of us spend a long time there and many get lost there, but to stay on the surface is stasis. Life itself usually forces us to descend, as we are often reluctant journeyers.

Many of the adults I have worked with dreamt, near the onset of therapy, of finding a new doorway in their home. It might open into a never-before known wing of their house or might lead to a stairway leading into an underground world. Rooms upon rooms and endless hallways may lead inwards or downwards, a virtual labyrinth of unexplored space. The dreamers are usually awestruck by the discovery, and at least for a moment there is a sense of life offering new possibilities, a realization of the unknown depth that is within them. How had they not known about this space before, they wonder upon awakening? While the truth of it still lingers, there is a feeling of great potential and even of grace.

Children readily access this same vast inner architecture via imaginative play. And this play too often involves a descent if it is allowed, especially when in the context of a therapeutic relationship. Play seems to always contain the possibility for children of finding a new way, of opening unopened doors. Yet its truth is not so fleeting for the child. They use new doorways and descend stairways into subterranean passageways fearlessly, protected by the safety of metaphor and the lack of an idea that it is wrong to do so. In doing so they tap unused energies and access unknown aspects of themselves that may change their lives.

As children move into adolescence they lose this ready and easy access to the depths as external life places ever-bigger demands on them as they grow. Deep rivers of physiological changes sweep the adolescent along leaving little time to linger and explore the psychic depths. Adolescents can and do feel things deeply and descend into the nether regions of their psyche and mine these for the gold that lies buried there. But their focus must also be to consider the importance and necessity of form.

For a brief period in childhood there is the ready possibility of exploring this deep inner space via imaginative play, using it to grow and also to heal. Form can fall apart and regroup in childhood without a sense of psychic disintegration. In the depth-oriented play therapy experience, the child is given materials to express and explore, permission to do so, and a guide who is willing to follow them and even lead when needed.

Parents often ask me if in the span of years I have practiced psychotherapy I have noticed a change in children. Are they fundamentally different now? Are the problems they face and the issues that they bring into treatment the same as always? Do they play differently? There is no simple answer to these questions. Children do seem to be wired differently than they were even 15 years ago. They certainly show more signs of sensory issues, learning disorders, attention issues, and other neurological problems and it is not just that therapists are simply more aware of these issues. They have increased and continue to do so. Today most children rarely have ready access to the outdoors and the unencumbered play that this allows. True play has almost vanished from schools and even from homes. All the vast amount of evidence for play's necessity has not affected how we educate or parent. For many children their first experience of spontaneous play comes in the play therapy space. The symptoms that brought them there may, in the end, seem like a blessing for the child uninitiated to play.

As test taking in schools becomes more important than actual learning, children have less chance to learn via the manipulation of material and form that manual play affords. They have grown up using electronic devices and often use these for a large number of hours each week. Even children who don't engage in electronic play are influenced by it as they live in a world that does. All these factors make for a different experience of childhood.

On the up side, children now use images with greater frequency in their play relating to the elements: earth, fire, water, and air. They use characters from mythology, influenced by television and/or video games but still offering the playing, imaginative child an interesting palette to choose from. This is a mixed blessing as it binds many children to following a script that is not theirs and not always that interesting. The smell of the marketed product is present in this play, but the creative therapist can do much to go deeper into these mythical images and use the potency that is latent there. If these images are used in the context of truly imaginative, rather than imitative, play they may readily become doorways.

The good news is that play is still the primary language of children and one that even the child who hasn't played before learns very quickly. It is still how young children learn best, even as play disappears from preschool programs. It is still the best way to speak with children, even as play disappears from child psychotherapy offices. I find that children readily leave their hand-held gaming devices, iPods, iPads, and so forth. in my waiting room, preferring the sandbox and the other materials my play space offers. They descend into the depths of play, often leaping in with both feet. And there is a need today more than ever for children to go deep in their use of play.

In treating children today, the old, simple psychotherapeutic formulas don't address the complexity that is the child. Perhaps they never really did. To only, or even mainly, see the child as part of a family system is not enough. It misses the deeper child. To view the child mainly in terms of the struggle of archetypes in the developing ego or to view a child only in terms of the patterns of chronic muscular tension that are developing is not enough. To consider how the child's behavior might be affected differently by how they think is not enough. These formulas miss the full child who is more than family dysfunction, muscular tension, thought patterns or archetypal imagery. The living child is much more than any of these formulaic visions, however compelling they may be.

What seems to make more and more sense to me is to offer children the potential to explore themselves fully as a member of a family, as an embodied being, as a thinking, feeling, aggressive, and imagining self, and more. If this happens in a safe space and in the context of a supportive relationship without limiting theories, without a preconceived idea of who the child is and/or must be, amazing things might happen. They might express their emotions, especially negative emotions, and the images these give rise to in the playing child without censorship. If they are not being told what to think, but rather offered play materials that can affect cognition and patterns of thought, their nascent thinking processes may expand. In such a setting, in which the child is allowed to play with aggressive impulses no matter how dysregulated they are, they may resolve deep issues and even enjoy doing so. They may move freely and loosen rigidity in their thinking or solidify their ability to process information as they discharge tensions in their bodies. They may become more regulated simply by being allowed to play with their dysregulation more deeply. Materials that allow ready use of the imagination in this setting are essential, as all of the above changes happen in children via imagination, especially if it is body centered. The evidence for this is confirmed by decades of research into the power of play.

For all children, maintaining a sense of integrity is of the utmost importance. They defend against the threat of disintegration even if their means of doing so seems dysfunctional. It helps to understand what is threatening the child's sense of integrity, and from where the problem is arising, within the child or their life situation. It is often the child's own organism that threatens them, that they are defending against, especially when there are neurological issues present. Getting to the bottom of the problem is key, rather than being symptom-focused. If we listen to what the symptoms are saying and try to see their root cause, their reason to be, we may really be able to help.

A seven-year-old girl once came for treatment due to a sudden manifestation of stress. She was increasingly echolalic (the tendency to echo one's own words) and fearful about a number of situations, especially in school. Peer relations had become problematic, leaving her often in tears. She struggled to accept the aggressive behavior of her peers. This behavior made her anxious, as her own aggressive impulses were inhibited by a highly developed sense of decorum. She was an unusually bright child, covertly competitive and a perfectionist. Her father described his own struggles with anxiety and periods of obsessive-compulsive behavior as a child. He felt that his daughter was wired similarly. Her younger sister had sensory issues and was quite oppositional. The daily difficulty this presented her parents with was also one part of the problem. She had to be "good" since her sister was so "bad." Yet her family and her school were open to her being less good. You could say her sense of integrity was threatened by her own inhibited aggression, stirred up in her but unable to express itself. For her, echolalia was a perfect manifestation of the problem, as much a symbol as a symptom. She couldn't assert but only echo. Yet she was at heart a very assertive but repressed child. Seeing it as such helped to resolve it quickly.

In her first session with me she drew herself as a monster whose body parts were completely mixed up. Her monster had several noses, several mouths and numerous eyes, all in odd places in the monster's body. Even its limbs were in the wrong places. The monster would not be a very effective monster given its jumbled state. But how sensitive and expressive this monster might be if he was organized, with all those eyes and noses and mouths! The drawing made her very happy.

She also spent time making her peers out of clay and pounding them to a pulp using a rubber hammer, tenuously at first but then with real gusto. This too made her very happy. She was readily able to forgo her usual sense of how things should be. The porosity of the child is such that even that which seems neurologically encoded can be altered if she is able to explore a new way of being. This may take a long while or it may happen quickly.

In the following session she created a world in the sandbox in which a girl lived in a lovely village with a deep moat surrounding it.

The village took up very little space in the box. As she described the world to me, she suddenly realized that this world she had made was quite limited. "I think the world really goes on much farther," she said with surprise. As she enlarged the world that the girl lived in she became very animated and emotional. She sensed and then alluded to the world beyond the moat, beyond the box, beyond the room and the building we were in. The box wasn't big enough to contain her expanding awareness.

Near the end of her play she whispered, "I think the world is endless!" She left amazed by the possibility that life was so much bigger than she thought. You could say that she too was a very big child trying to diminish her own bigness, trying to fit in. Suddenly she allowed her consciousness and her energy to release. After this session her echolalia ceased and her anxiety began to abate. Accessing her buried aggression playfully enabled her vision and her sense of self to expand. Articulating this via her sandplay and via her words furthered this. There was no part of the child left out of this experience; body, mind, emotions, imagination were all engaged. And the willingness of her family and teachers to welcome a more assertive child helped immensely.

This book is not intended as a simple homage to play. It is rather an exploration by its authors of their experience of playing in an in-depth approach that is both grounded in theory and yet "out of the box", often quite literally. These seasoned therapists combine solid training as psychotherapists with the capacity to see beyond the confines of the old methods, the old ideologies. They embrace the necessity of widening the lens with which we view children, even as we look deeper into what is happening as the child explores and expresses via play. The age range of the therapists/authors is remarkable, spanning nearly fifty years. That there are six male therapists contributing is also remarkable in a branch of psychotherapy that has always been mainly women.

The book begins by exploring the play of a primitive tribe in Malaysia, whose life is an array of playing that ensures bonding and the forging of connections to each other and the natural and spiritual world. This chapter is an anthropological study of the all-encompassing play of this tribe and forms a portal for the rest of the book, most of which takes place in play therapy spaces in which play and play materials dissolve and then reform as the child does so. The final chapter explores an in-depth approach to therapy with adults, added here since all children become adults, often carrying burdens from their childhood with them. It is interesting to consider how as adults our dream life is in fact imaginative play, helping us access deeper parts of ourselves and psyches like play does.

As the world both expands and contracts through the use of technology at an ever-increasing speed, we need to consider how to help children live in it. This is true for all children but especially true for children who enter treatment. How do we help them maintain their integrity and their connection to self that is already ruptured or threatened? How do we help them struggle to become conscious? The methods we use in treatment and the world view we have of both the child and of life itself play an important role in this process. In order to be an effective clinician today we need to be a philosopher, an archaeologist, and a seeker. And we must be willing and able to play deeply and trust this as the way forward.

CHAPTER ONE

A Deep Story of Deep Play

How the Play, Trance and Séance of the Senoi Temiar People Can Help us Understand Greater Playfulness

Dr. Sue Jennings

And they shall fetch thee jewels from the deep
W. Shakespeare, *A Midsummer Night's Dream* (iii.1.161)

Introduction

> From the first moments of our lives, we exist within a complex matrix of social relationships. This elaborate social relatedness is organised and controlled by neural networks of bonding and attachment, play, predicting others intentions and being to see the world through others eyes. (Cozolino 2002, p.172)

The focus of my work, research, and writing is play and playfulness. Cozolino, as he states above, integrates the important threads of play and neuroscience into new understanding of human social relationships. He increases our grasp of what we understand as "deep play". Therefore the main thrust of this chapter is to reflect on the variations of play and playfulness, together with what we experience as deep play. As there are many fragmented approaches to and understandings of deep play, I am using my ethnographic knowledge of the Senoi Temiar people as an overview of a whole life deep play experience. Playfulness for these people is integrated into their life cycle, and there are key moments, usually associated with dangerous life transitions, where deep play can be observed.

"Deep play" appears to mean different things to different people and people who do playwork or child psychotherapy or child anthropology studies will talk about deep play in different ways. Sutton-Smith (2001) suggests that "deep play" is risky play and includes activities such as caving, hang-gliding, skate boarding and rafting. In his seminal book *The Ambiguity of Play*, he has produced a detailed taxonomy of play terms and categories.

He later suggests that modern forms of play are the ones where "people talk about psychological development, the imagination, and the subjectivity of the agent – the self" and:

> Then we get the ancient ones, which have been around much longer. The main one is all about contests, but also there are play forms which are about membership, and some that are about risk – gambling, and jumping off mountains, parachuting and so on. And finally there is nonsense and that's for the tricksters. (Sutton-Smith, interviewed by Michael Patte in Brown and Patte 2013, p.16)

Brown (2008) suggests that play and playwork theory has focussed on psychological, biological, and evolutionary models of play at the expense of sociological and developmental models. Brown emphasises the importance of the play in itself, not only the learning through play. I agree that the direct experience of play, and also drama, are important for health as well as therapy.

Child psychotherapists and play therapists also look for depth in the play of children; however, there are those who look for depth in the therapeutic relationship contrasted with those who look for depth in the play.

Anthropologist Clifford Geertz (1973) applies the term deep play to his observations of a cock fight in Bali. He describes how the term was probably first used by Jeremy Bentham (Fuller 1964, p.432) to define play in which the stakes are so high that it is irrational to participate (p.432). Bentham says that such play should be made illegal (and those concerned with gambling addiction would probably agree). However, as Geertz points out, in the cock fight which has virtually matching high stakes, there is something more profound going on: it is symbolic of the Balinese sense of self and status. The question is therefore, what is going on in deep play?

For playworker and anthropologist alike there is a sense of risk and danger, and perhaps therapists would also argue that therapy involves personal risk of the self. If we look at examples of deep play it may be possible to find a meeting point between all approaches, especially in our playwork with children.

One way of looking at deep play is the degree to which the child is absorbed in their play activity. Deep absorption we know about as adults, when we are reading a book and do not notice the fire has gone out or that light is fading outside; we suddenly become aware that we are cold and have difficulty in seeing.

In this chapter I hope to create some coherence between the cultural expectations of deep play for the individual as well as deep play for the culture as a whole. Many of the action techniques of dramatic play (Jennings 2014a) enable children and teenagers to rehearse the skills and trust necessary for having a deep play experience. For this I will draw upon research with the Temiar peoples of Malaysia and my later exploration of neuroscience in the practice of Neuro-Dramatic-Play.

The Senoi Temiars

The Temiars are a tribal people who inhabit the rapidly disappearing rain forest in the Malay Peninsula. They are subject to increasing incursion by the dominant class, the governing Malays, and are under pressure to convert to Islam. Traditionally they are settled cultivators, planting hill rice, foraging for vegetables and fruit, and hunting edible animals and fish. They are non-violent and non-competitive, and cosmic danger is from Tiger and Thunder. Human danger is from foreigners. They are child-centred and spend lengthy time massaging and stroking infants and small children. Children are not allowed on the ground until they can walk independently (they live in stilt houses off the ground); the ground is the realm of animals and most animals are either dirty or dangerous. Their developmental stages are: child – young adult – older adult; there is no obvious adolescent stage.

Temiars have well developed ideas about being playful: play is related to dreams, and the playful and healing séances. Their séances are events involving singing, dancing, and various degrees of trance, for which they often use the word to forget. Usually, the largest house in the village is where the séance will take place and will have decorations from leaves and flowers, depending on the seriousness and scale of the séance. Some "sing-ins", as they are called, are for fun and play, others are more serious and for healing or because individual adults really enjoy the trance experience. The belief behind the séance is that the spirit guides can be called down through song and will dispense healing energy through the shaman (Jennings 1995, Benjamin 2014).

Children may play at being the different roles that occur in the séance, outside or underneath the house, wearing discarded headdresses or decorations. Children will also play at being in trance during the main séances after the main healing and trance has taken place. The Temiars also describe the singing and dancing sessions as playing. Trance is not the main focus, and the sessions are a culmination of vigorous singing and dancing to the accompaniment of bamboo stompers. Sometimes adults will ask them to keep the noise down, and even invoke the Thunder and Tiger malevolent entities who might just intervene if they are too noisy! These playful sessions are also an opportunity for flirting and for hopeful shamans to try out their skills.

There is a more serious but still playful version of the "sing-in", which they explained was to keep the village healthy, to keep the "head-soul" of the village strong. There may be some spontaneous trance and impromptu healing by the local shaman.

Designated healing séances are more elaborate in their decorations and organisations. The shaman may go into trance in order to facilitate a cure, other people may spontaneously go into trance. Older people go into trance with little physical movement, just a little rocking and rubbing their faces with their leaf fans. Younger people will be much more energetic, jumping, falling, leaping and often collapsing on the bamboo floor, (for a more detailed description see Jennings 1995). Usually the whole village attends and most people stay until dawn.

The deeper séances are often organised when there has been illness in the village or a family may request one for a sick family member. The shaman may decide it would be a good thing: the feelings of goodwill are always noticeable after a deep and heavy trance session.

These sessions are longed for by the Temiars and sorely missed by them during the mourning period when they are forbidden. The trance is very much linked to the dream and in both states one can discover new songs and dances, cures, and fertile land. Through dreaming one acquires a playful spirit guide who brings knowledge and information. These séances are one form of deep play in the Geertz sense of the word. The Tiger Séance, described below, is another strong and more complex example of deep play.

Geertz (1973) describes the deep play of the Balinese people demonstrated through their traditional cock fights. Cock fights, although illegal, are very popular in Bali as an expression of cultural and community identity; the Balinese are aware of the double meaning of the word cock: the real penis and the symbolic penis. The cock fights are dramas in social life that are symbolic of the issues in day-to-day life; they express the aggression that otherwise could not be shown. The cock fight is about status and prestige, not about the financial gain as the bets are more or less evenly matched. Furthermore, Geertz describes the antipathy the Balinese have towards animals, often showing gratuitous violence towards their dogs. In their scale of values bestiality is considered worse than incest. Therefore the Balinese identification with their cock is also allowing them to connect with their darkness, their most hated and feared entity: what we could also term their shadow-self.

A similar paradox exists for the Temiars in regard to the Tiger Séance. Tiger is to be feared and avoided and children are taught a fear response to Tiger from birth. When I asked one man where he was going as he left the village with a blow-pipe, he promptly came back and said he would go another day, as Tiger might have overheard our conversation. The Temiars always have Tiger stories to tell when inside the house and sitting in close proximity and speaking in hushed tones. When I told them about the children's game "What's the time Mr. Wolf?" they suggested we could play it saying "Mr. Tiger": a new way of reinforcing the fear of Tiger through play. When major taboos are broken the belief is that people are punished by Tiger who is all seeing and all powerful. Tiger is never mentioned by name unless the Malay word is used.

I suggest that the Tiger Séance, healing at its most dangerous, is the deep play of the Temiars. It is only performed by the highest of the shaman who are designated to be a Tiger shaman, usually one in each river valley. It means that the shaman has been able to have Tiger as a spirit guide, whereas lesser shamans have shy flower sprites as their spirit guides. This is the paradox: that the most feared and dangerous animal has become the helper of the shaman.

Because the energy that generates from the Tiger is believed to be extremely dangerous, the proceedings are strictly controlled in near darkness. There is no dance at a Tiger Séance. A small shelter is built from branches of attap; there is a chorus of female singers, beating out a duple rhythm with bamboo stompers and singing in response to the shaman's assistant. He acts like a stage manager and makes sure that everything is in its place: anyone in need of healing lies on the floor near the shelter, incense is burning near the fire and fresh flowers are placed outside the shelter. The lights are dimmed and the shaman crawls inside the shelter. The intensity of the singing increases and everyone jumps as a scratching sounds on the inside of the shelter. This indicates that the shaman has actually metamorphosed into Tiger and his claws are scratching the attap; soon he starts to growl and the audience sit very tense and scared. The shaman's assistant continues singing, building the intensity as the scratching and growling increases, suddenly he stops, the music stops and the lights go up as the shaman is seen to disappear out of the shelter and the house. The deeper the play the more restricted and controlled is the space, light and participation.

The assistant shows us that the flowers are all wilted proving that the energy of the Tiger has been strong. The unwell people gradually "wake-up" and say they are feeling better; unlike the ordinary healing séances, touch is not allowed in the Tiger Séance, as the energy is believed to be too powerful! Anyone who has been affected can smell the incense and waft it over their face and head. The singing slowly reverts to the ordinary séance singing. Eventually the shaman returns to the house, smells the incense and smokes the ritual cigarettes that have been placed for him. He looks exhausted. In the three Tiger Séances that I observed there was little verbal communication from the shaman after the event – he seemed in a process of recovery. Other people would talk about the Tiger and how they saw the claws disappear as the lights went up. Sometimes an ordinary séance will follow the Tiger Séance once the shelter and wilted flowers have been removed. Often it is another shaman who will lead the later séance.

By contrast, in the more general healing séances the shaman will often tell the story of the journey that his head-soul had to make to fetch a cure or find a new dance step or song. Healing, creativity, and play happen at several levels for the Temiars and they can often move through the levels on the same occasion, with the exception of the Tiger Séance.

Temiar healing

The Temiars have a very clear idea of activities that are for prevention and those that are for cure. They are also very aware that the head-soul of the village and of the individual must be kept strong. Small babies have a very weak head-soul and might slip away so their heads are kept covered and they stay in the house until they can walk (unless carried on the back of an adult). Parents of small children do not go into trance because their child's head-soul relies on the head-soul of the parents. Similarly, people who are unwell and seeking healing do not go into trance as it might further weaken their head-soul. When someone has died then the whole community will enter a period of mourning when no one leaves the village and there are no séances. When the mourning period ends there is a special séance with music in a minor key and it is the bereaved relatives that go into trance.

So there is continuity between the private world of dreaming, where you might meet your spirit guide or your playmate, and the play of children who play out adult situations, including the trance sessions, both on their own as well as in the group séance. There is a continued spectrum of greater physical control and rules of performance which culminate in the most dangerous and the most controlled Tiger Séance. This is where healing and danger come together for powerful effect.

Deep attachment

Child birth is a very closed, confined experience with the mother, infant, and midwife staying together during the post-partum period. The new infant is constantly being massaged and breast-feeding is on demand. Once the midwife leaves, the father slowly begins to figure more in the care of the child and shares the birth name of the child (both parents are known by the gender of the first born: parents of a boy or parents of a girl – in case there is any confusion, they add on the name of the child. So parents are known by the name of their children). A deep attachment is created and maintained until the child can walk independently, through:

- close proximity and massage between parents and infant
- shared soul protection of infant as no trance for parents
- shared names between parents and child
- shared food taboos between parents.

However, although their parents do not trance, small babies after the post-partum time attend the séances in slings on their mother's chest or back. Usually mothers and older teenage girls beat out a strong rhythm with bamboo stompers on a log, echoing the songs of the shaman. The child is embedded in the rhythm, cadences, dance, smells, and physicality of the séance, as well as the close proximity of massage and attachment with the parents – a strong basis for Neuro-Dramatic-Play.

Neuro-Dramatic-Play

My original developmental paradigm "Embodiment-Projection-Role", which I have developed for over 30 years, charts the play and drama development of children from birth to 7 years; it has formed the basis of many therapeutic interventions and educational programmes across the world. In recent years I conducted additional research on the embodiment stage, realising it needed more fine-tuning. McCarthy (2007) recommends a "body-centred" approach to play therapy, yet many play therapists do not allow touch or feel comfortable using a body-centred way of working. I extended the embodied starting point to six months before birth and charted the sensory – rhythmic – dramatic play (including stories), as a deeper awareness of embodiment growth; attention is also paid to the "as-if" (or dramatic act), the moment within a few hours of birth, when the infant tries to imitate the expression on the mother's face. Although western babies have less confinement and physicality compared with the Temiars, nevertheless Neuro-Dramatic-Play (NDP) can be observed with the pre-pregnancy, child birth, and post-pregnancy attachment and sensory play, heartbeats and changes of expression. However, there are increasing numbers of children who do not experience physical attachment and sensory experience (Jennings, 2011, 2013). Jennings (2014b) includes many body-based techniques to contain and transform children's difficulties which prevent them from deep play experiences. The NDP stages can be observed in the development of infants all over the world, and appear to serve as a deep play experience that precedes more complex cultural and social development. Cozolino (2008) suggests that it is safe to assume that the transposition of maternal attention into brain structure occurs in the human brain: "These and many more findings drive home the fact that the brain is a social organ, built at the interface between experience and genetics, where nature and nurture become one" (p.45). Louis Cozolino has written extensively on the relationship of neuroscience and therapy (2008, 2006, 2002).

The Temiars' cycle

The importance of the Temiars' story is that there is a continuity of child rearing, socialisation, and adult healing practice that integrates the community as well as the individuals within it. The organisation is with both body and space. There is a clear boundary between home space and outside space, and between the outside space and the wild space of the forest. There are rules of who is allowed to enter which space, such as children not being allowed outside until they can walk. Only adult males are allowed to go into deep jungle for hunting animals; these animals are considered dangerous, either to hunt or to eat, and are surrounded by taboos. Women and teenage girls go as far as the jungle fringes to forage and gather, and also to the rice field to weed, plant, and harvest. Since the Temiars live in stilt houses, the spaces are divided up both horizontally as well as vertically (in the house or outside, and on and off the ground). The river is also important in space as Temiars have their sense of direction from the river: upstream, downstream, across the bank (Benjamin 1967). The river is used for washing people and clothes, and as the loo, so the bank is divided into clear zones; the river is also a play-space for children of all ages and the outside space where there is greatest freedom. Adults, especially older women, may suggest they play less noisily or boisterously as thunder might notice (similarly with the lively play-séances). Contrasted with the containment of the land spaces, there is a sense of the flow of the river. One shaman suggested that a baby was late in arrival because the mother's bed was facing up river instead of down!

There are four deep experiences that are most contained. They are child birth, where a small room with the fire is either built or boarded off from the living area of the house and there are strict rules of who can enter and what happens to blood and placenta. The second is the shelter that the adult men construct in the forest if they need to sleep overnight. One would expect it to be away from danger but it is a small shelter on the ground made of branches leaning against each other. Symbolically a forest nature hut as contrasted with the village houses or group dwellings. The third confined space is the shelter build by the Tiger Shaman for the séance. This is built by men within the bigger space of the village house. There are also rules of not only who can enter these spaces but also what may be carried into the space. For example, animal meat that has strong taboos attached must be taken into the nearest house to the forest. Fourth, there is the confined space after death. Bodies are wrapped in cloth and bamboo mats immediately after death and are carried across the river and buried. It is believed that spirits of the dead cannot cross water. The grave is referred to as a house and it is left with lights to keep wild animals away.

The body rules govern what goes into the body, what comes out of it, and where. Covering up the body is from the waist down unless strangers are about. There are beliefs that the head-soul lodges on top of the head and the blood-soul lodges vaguely at the base of the sternum. There are rules about which animals can be consumed and at what age. Fruit, grown vegetables, and rice do not have taboos but on the ground animals do have rules. For more detail see Jennings (1995) and Benjamin (2014).

At any one time the Temiars know what their body should be doing and in which space.

Integration of deep play and story and Neuro-Dramatic-Play

Sensory, rhythmic, and dramatic play are deep play markers in the early development of children. Temiar children are able to be physically 'attached' to their mothers, as well as emotionally held from birth onwards. Since breastfeeding lasts several years on demand, it is rare to see a distressed child. Rhythmic play is not only connected to heart beats with the mother, but to the infant's experience of the trance sessions where their mother is playing the bamboo stompers and the rhythms permeate the bamboo walls and floor, as well as being felt through the singing bodies.

Dramatic play and stories happen through the playful interactions between parents, siblings, and through massage and story. The Temiars also have more formal storytelling that is an activity in its own right. Stories are used to give examples of inappropriate behaviour through metaphors; time will be spent re-telling their creation myths. Stories may also be shared from a dream experience. The more formal storytelling is never done on the same night as singing and dancing. But they will always sit and listen to a yarn, especially if it comes from a dream. It is almost unheard of in traditional Temiar families for parents to hit their children. Parents, unlike Tiger and Thunder, are loving and indulgent, and if mother isn't available, it will be grandmother who will comfort the child and also tell stories.

All the stages of NDP are very intensive in the early life of Temiar children with strong holding and attached relationships. Just as the start of life is sheltered, focused, and intense, the end of life is detached and separated, and can be carried out by strong friends rather than close relatives.

The deep play experience is present throughout the life cycle of the Temiars and can be seen as an integrated cultural phenomenon. It is present at child birth and early child raising, during dreaming and playing, in séances, and healing. It is physically imprinted on Temiar individuals as well as collectively in the village or community.

Being able to experience this integration when I lived with the tribe for eighteen months, was helpful in bridging across disciplines and professions in our play endeavours. We are all aware of the notion of splitting in our therapeutic play work, but perhaps it can be better understood if we can integrate deep play into our personal life cycle as well as our interdisciplinary dialogues.

We have much to learn from the Temiar people.

References

Benjamin, G. (1967) *Temiar Religion*. Unpublished PhD thesis, University of Cambridge.

Benjamin, G. (2014) *Temiar Religion, 1964–2012: Enchantment, Disenchantment, and Re-enchantment in Malaysia's Uplands*. Singapore, China: NUS Press.

Brown, F. (2008) "The Fundamentals of Playwork" in Brown F. and Taylor C. (eds) *Foundations of Playwork*. Maidenhead, UK: Open University Press.

Brown, F. and Patte, M. (2013) *Rethinking Children's Play*. London, UK: Bloomsbury.

Cozolino, L. (2002) *The Neuroscience of Psychotherapy: Building and Re-building the Human Brain*. New York, NY: W.W. Norton.

Cozolino, L. (2006) *The Neuroscience of Human Relationships: Attachment and the Developing Social Brain*. New York, NY: W.W. Norton.

Cozolino, L. (2008) *The Healthy Ageing Brain: Sustaining Attachment, Attaining Wisdom*. New York, NY: W.W. Norton.

Fuller, L.L. (1964) *The Morality of Law*. New Haven, CT: International Library of Psychology.

Jennings, S. (1995) *Theatre, Ritual and Transformation: The Senoi Temiars of Malaysia*. Hove, UK: Routledge.

Jennings, S. (2011) *Healthy Attachments and Neuro-Dramatic-Play*. London, UK: Jessica Kingsley Publishers.

Jennings, S. (2014b) *101 Ideas for Focus and Motivation*. Buckingham, UK: Hinton House.

Jennings, S. (2014a) *101 Ideas for Positive Thoughts and Feelings*. Buckingham, UK: Hinton House.

Geertz, C. (1973) *The Interpretation of Cultures*. New York, NY: Basic Books.

Jennings, S. (2013) *101 Ideas for Managing Challenging Behaviour*. Buckingham, UK: Hinton House.

McCarthy, D. (2007) *If You Turned into a Monster.* London, UK: Jessica Kingsley Publishers.

Sutton-Smith, B. (2001) *The Ambiguity of Play.* London, UK and Cambridge MA: Harvard University Press.

Shakespeare, W. *A Midsummer Night's Dream.* London, UK: Penguin.

Sutton-Smith (2013) Interview by M. Patte in F. Brown and M. Patte (eds) *Rethinking Children's Play.* London, UK: Bloomsbury.

CHAPTER TWO

Journeying Within

Using Tunnel and Cave Imagery to Access the Inner Imaginative World

Timothy Rodier

There once was a city. Seemingly ordinary with its buildings, cars, and streets, this city actually had an extraordinary attraction. At the edge of the city limits, a magical tunnel, called The Portal, led to another world.

All the city's residents wanted access to this other world. However, at the mouth of The Portal stood a powerful guardian. With his lightning bolt staff, he struck down all residents unworthy to enter The Portal. Only those who had lived in the city for many years, who were mature in age, and could withstand a zap from the lightning bolt were granted access to the other world. Residents who passed this test were given a key to The Portal and had unlimited access to the other dimension.

In order to transport the city's residents, The Portal needed energy from the Power Crystal. However, the Power Crystal required frequent recharging and needed to be taken to the center of the city to be reenergized. The residents guarded the Power Crystal and charging station very seriously as they understood the important role they played in The Portal's vitality. It was the people's role to protect them.

As the city grew older, more and more people were given keys to the other dimension, therefore more keys were needed.

Eventually, the other world became overcrowded, and the people of the city needed to make more and more keys, and rapidly. But the new keys were not as good as the original keys; they would lose power quickly and required constant recharging. The need for effective keys and recharging began to occupy the people's minds. Wars broke out as they tried to steal each other's keys. Everyone wanted more power. Some people devised a plan to capture the Power Crystal and charging station located in the center of the city. The Portal guardian, disgusted with the people's greed and behavior, came into the city and destroyed everyone.

This story may seem like a modern day myth, with its commentary on the downfall of our society, where power, greed, and technology take the driver's seat in occupying our minds and time. It speaks to the increasing need for power, not just in obtaining our personal goals and living out our aspirations, but also for the devices that run our lifestyles and keep us organized. The true lesson is that we are less concerned with our authentic experience and the importance of tradition and rite of passage, and more focused on the leg-up we can gain over others and the impatient quick-fix. And of course, the story has an ending of biblical proportions, where the True and All Powerful entity punishes the reckless sinners, and at the end of the day, reminds us that we truly are powerless.

As adults, we can easily draw the analytic parallels between this narrative and our modern times. However, when my client Matthew, a ten-year-old boy diagnosed with Asperger's Syndrome, created this story he called "The Portal" using two sandboxes in my office, I knew we were on the verge of a shift in his treatment. Up until this point, Matthew's play was rigid, inflexible, and repetitive. He would often make roads, perfectly smooth, steady, and level, that did not lead anywhere. At my suggestion he created the tunnel, which led to this narrative.

We can read The Portal as a contemporary parable, but perhaps the themes also reflect more about Matthew's own difficulties in negotiating his two worlds. He managed to play two very different roles in his life: controlled and polite at school and in our sessions, and then rageful, obstinate, crude, and vulgar at home. He was misunderstood by his parents, who were divided in their approach to Matthew's outbursts. His father lost his own temper. His mother dismissed Matthew's behavior because of his diagnoses. Matthew was prescribed mood stabilizers, anti-depressants, and stimulants for his co-morbid ADHD.

After creating The Portal, Matthew allowed himself to access his emotions in our sessions, in particular anger. He quickly became more physically active and rough in his play. Yelling, screaming, and cursing, he discharged his repressed emotions, which cleared a path for more genuine communion and relationship with the unconscious. In my office, he was able to safely pass out of the world in which he needed to be sane, organized, and rigid and enter into the world where he was able to lash out, and test the boundaries of his rage in a safe environment. It felt as if my office became his Portal.

As therapists, we need to pay attention to the parallel between digging deep to create caves and tunnels and digging deep into oneself to create an outlet for the unconscious. This profound process should be honored, especially with children. Utilizing the techniques of dynamic play therapy in my work, the imagery of tunnels and caves has helped my clients better access their imagination and creativity, which often leads to deepening our exploration. I have often noticed that when a new client first approaches the sandbox, it seems like a natural gesture to dig a hole in the sand, essentially creating a cave. Frequently, the cave will turn into a tunnel as the child seeks an exit (Figure 2.1, page 40). Taking their techniques, I began to provoke the creation of tunneling into play with many of my clients, which I noticed created a level of engagement with the imagination that helped their unconscious become more available in our sessions. It seems as though the deeper they tunnel, the deeper they can access their inner world and make discoveries about their identities and emotional layers.

Of course, this is true with other materials besides sand. I observed with awe as eight-year-old Eric used clay to non-verbally process his reaction to his father's aggression. Unprompted, Eric silently and methodically molded the clay into a cave, then opened the other side into a tunnel, and finally added details to create a sort of ribcage structure (Figure 2.2). I wondered if his creation reflected his desire to protect himself, mainly his heart, from the fear of unpredictable violent behavior from his father.

Figure 2.1: From Cave to Tunnel

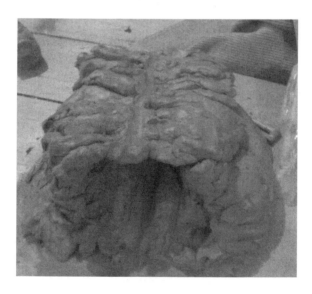

Figure 2.2: Eric's Ribcage Tunnel

Observing the frequency of this strong symbolism has prompted an exploration into our history of tunnels and caves. What is it about these images that they continue to reappear in my work with clients? On some level, my clients are able to tap into the collective and common experience and use these images, in essence, to provide an opening for an emergence into new territory.

Throughout literature, mythology, and fairy tales, tunnels and caves have long represented mysterious and enchanting places that harbor secrets, provide protection, and lead protagonists to other dimensions. Alice found a Wonderland on the other side of the rabbit hole, chasing curiosity and dealing with growing up. A seemingly ordinary wardrobe leads four curious siblings into the world of Narnia. It was in the darkness of a cave where Bilbo Baggins stumbled upon the Ring of Binding Power that held the course of good and evil. Luke Skywalker is beckoned into a dark tree cave while training to become a Jedi. Luke inquires about what dwells in the darkness of the cave. Yoda replies that he will only face what he brings with him. In the cave he confronts his fear and anger, truly beginning his Jedi training. The journey into the dark unknown of the cave and into the depth of the tunnel is the place to discover our truth.

Prior to contemporary literature, the image of the transformative power of these deep spaces is present in ancient mythology and religious texts as well. Considered sacred places, caves have been described as a portal to the gods. Homer writes in The Odyssey about a mysterious cave that has two entrances; one used for men and the other for the gods. Early Christian texts describe caves as both a womb and a tomb, where Christ was born in a cave manger, and then later laid in the cave tomb upon his death, which becomes the space for his transformation into his resurrected state. In a Hymn in Praise of Wisdom in the book of Job 28:3, 10–11:

> Man makes an end to darkness when he pierces to the utmost depths the black and lightless rock…driving tunnels through the rocks on the watch for anything precious. He explores the sources of rivers and brings to daylight secrets that were hidden.

Although Job later states that true wisdom comes from faith in God, this verse still highlights the human quest to seek out our secrets in dark places. Saint Francis, a monk in 1200 A.D., sought hermitage in the caves above Assisi where he and his brother friars stripped themselves of all possessions and sought solitude as a means to discover God and Self.

From early human history, caves and tunnels have served as a refuge and sanctuary. In these places of complete darkness, our ancestors sought shelter, worshiped and honored gods with prayerful drawings for successful hunts, and buried their dead with ritualistic practices. The solace of the cave provided an environment to commune with the spiritual in a protected and safe space.

Children, for the most part, are unaware of the historical, spiritual, and cultural significance of caves and tunnels, yet these images still frequent therapeutic play spaces. It seems as if children instinctually seek hidden and protected spaces in their play. In his book *Children's Special Places* (1993), David Sobel wrote of the importance of children finding their safe space and creative outlet for transformation.

> During this period of middle childhood, the self is fragile and under construction and needs to be protected from view of the outside world. The secretive nature of the hiding place is significant. The self, like the metamorphosing larva of the butterfly, needs to be wrapped in a cocoon before it emerges into the light. Thus, the places that children seek out are places where they cannot be seen, places to begin the unfolding of the self. (p.70)

In a way, children are in a constant birthing process as new aspects of themselves form and then surface. Throughout their development, children's identities start to take shape and their egos are maturing; the self is emerging. The caves and tunnels created in children's play may be a functional expression of the need to find a sacred space to grow.

Contrary to adults, children move rapidly through stages of development, shifting physically and emotionally into exciting, but sometimes terrifying, experiences of themselves and their world. Erich Neumann, a psychoanalyst and writer who studied with Carl Jung, theorized that a major developmental task is traversing the journey from what he called the "psychological matriarch," which is that time from infancy and the security of the "primal" relationship, to the "psychological patriarch," in which we are initiated into the world and society (Neumann 1973). This shifting away from the security of the parental relationship is crucial for a child's healthy adjustment into society and experiences outside the family. It is also necessary for the individual's emotional and psychological development in support of a healthy identity and self-concept. Unfortunately, there is much interference in our society that does not support this process. As therapists, our role is to guide our clients towards a healthy transition into the stage of Neumann's psychological patriarch. Peter, a seven-year-old client, used my play space to create several worlds in which to help him move through his developmental stages away from his overbearing mother to assimilate into experiences beyond this complicated relationship.

Despite his small stature and babyish features, Peter often lashed out brutally towards his mother, kicking and biting her during their arguments. Peter's father generally played a passive role, except when Peter's mother forced him to present with a unified front. Peter's mother found it extremely difficulty to release any control. In our first session, she allowed Peter to come in to my office alone. Although she remained in the waiting room, his mother turned off the sound machine and listened at the door. For the next few sessions, she requested to remain in the play space with Peter, so I tried to engage her in the play. Together the three of us created sand scenes, drew pictures, and attempted to play, but his mom showed difficulty in letting her guard down to engage authentically. In order to access Peter's creative self, I knew I needed him to feel that he had command of the space without his mother's presence.

In our first session without his mother in the room, Peter quickly made his way to the toy soldiers and began to construct a battleground in the sandbox. The parallel between the war he created and the conflict at home was immediately clear. I also noticed that he played on the surface, in that he did not utilize the depth of the sandbox.

In our next session, Peter spontaneously created a tunnel. As he dug deep into the sandbox, he described the tunnel as a dangerous place because a monster lived inside. We spent the session carefully considering our method for dealing with the tunnel monster, from luring it out to attacking it, and then eventually deciding to trick the monster to come out of the tunnel by thinking we had befriended it. When we extracted the monster, we were able to begin exploring the worlds that existed through the tunnel.

In our play, there were always four worlds and our exploration consistently started the same. He selected two figures, typically a knight or soldier, to be the main characters, one for me and one for him. The third character, also played by Peter, was hapless and expendable, sort of the comic relief, and would sometimes die in the play. The story started in the first world, with our figurines hiding behind a military bunker spying on the monster, which could be a giant or a dragon, and one time he chose a mother goddess figurine. Our characters would trick and defeat the monster or sometimes we would sneak around it and then go into the tunnel.

We would then move into the other sandbox to enter into the second world, a mysterious and magical place where unexplainable events occurred. The theme in this world was survival and escape. We were always lost and our weapons had malfunctioned. After setting up camp and making a fire, we would meet another character that could tell us the hidden secrets about this world. Here, the space could easily change and morph to the confusion of our characters. Plants and trees would suddenly appear. The sand around us would shift and change the landscape, much to our surprise. Frequently, we were faced with obstacles to overcome, like a den of dragons, quicksand, statues that had come alive to chase us, and vines that had grown around us and were trying to drag us away. We always left this world in a panic, attempting to escape whatever was hunting us. Once we found the tunnel, sometimes having to dig to find it, we were always relieved to have made it out alive.

Panting and breathless, we would stumble into the third world in the Victorian dollhouse. Our characters would walk around the house, wondering how to get inside. Suddenly, the bathroom set would appear on the front lawn. Although we were always struck by the strangeness, we would all enjoy a moment to relax in the tub. Then, several naked baby figures would come over to use the toilet. They would urinate and defecate all over, sometimes even on my character. Peter's character always worried about the babies because no one was watching them. A man, the grandfather doll, was supposed to be taking care of the babies, but was not paying attention. We would then decide to climb into the house through the window. Each time as we were about to open the window, Peter's character would smash it to break in. My character would act surprised and Peter would respond, "Aw, c'mon, it's fun!" We would then walk around the inside of the house, talking about the rooms and furniture, until we realized that the grandfather doll was trying to destroy us. We would spend our time hiding from him while trying to find the tunnel to escape.

We then would emerge into the last world, my office. At this point we would abandon our characters and just be ourselves, but we acted as if we were discovering the space for the first time. We would marvel at all the figures, clay, and toys in the office and wondered together for what the space was used. It was here, in my office world that we could actually talk about the issues with his parents and the dynamics at home.

We played out this story for months, rarely veering from our script. On one level it felt as if Peter seemed stuck, unable to move beyond these scenes. While initially tempted to modify the play, I began to recognize that his scenes in each of the worlds were communicating a need to traverse his relationship with his parents and himself. Like a reoccurring dream, we had much to learn from the metaphors that we played out each week. Peter needed to unearth and confront his monsters, and learn to maneuver and plot escape from a life where the unpredictable environment posed a threat. I wondered if the babies and the negligent caregiver reflected his regressive behaviors, and that he may need a stronger presence of male role models in his life at this stage of his development. And finally, the moment of arriving to present time as ourselves, without the guise of our characters, where we shared the experience of newness and wonder of the therapy office. In this manner, he was not entering into treatment alone; he created a world where it was new and unknown to me as well. Here, we solidified our authentic experience together and were able to face each other, as our true selves (see Figure 2.3).

Figure 2.3: Soldiers Getting Ready to Confront

Over the course of these play sessions, I met with his parents on a regular basis and was able to understand the nature of the conflict and the family dynamics. Peter was trapped, trying to negotiate the extremes between his father's immature behavior and his mother's intense rage. While the treatment helped him negotiate a passage between these extremes within himself, an initial goal focused on helping his mother leave the sound machine on during our sessions. It was important she understood that trusting Peter to be alone in the therapy office with me also conveyed a trust in his ability to begin to navigate the world outside his family. Not surprisingly, the day that Peter chose the mother goddess as the tunnel monster was the same day that his mother finally left the sound machine on. By extricating the monster from the tunnel, Peter could now access the passage to the parts of himself that needed to emerge.

Using tunnel imagery can allow for the unearthing of one's hidden desires. Such is the case with Sam, a seven-year-old involved in treatment to help minimize anxiety due to his sensory processing disorder. A conscientious and thoughtful boy, he was very curious about my personal life and would frequently ask about my family, especially my children. Despite his sweet disposition, his play always focused on destruction. Whether with physical play or a sand scene, the story would quickly end with his victorious annihilation of any other characters.

Sam's small body contained enormous anger towards the areas in his life that he felt were unfair. His mother was often unavailable to him as she was busy with his younger sibling's frequent treatments for a serious illness. Sam was not allowed to touch his sibling for fear of injury. He frequently made negative and belittling statements about himself at school and home and generally presented with low self-esteem. His school did not understand his need to engage physically; he was frequently ostracized by his peers and would be punished for physical activity that was misinterpreted as aggressive.

Figure 2.4: Sam's China

While the destruction theme allowed him to access and discharge this anger, it also felt necessary to help him access the transformative power of turning destruction to creation. While constructing a sand scene involving a battle against a dragon with mass carnage of the soldiers and uncontrollable fires, I asked him to create a tunnel. As he dug into the sand, Sam described the tunnel as an escape that led to another world. Moving to the other sandbox, he created a world he called "China" that resembled a Zen garden with ponds, fish, pandas, and a temple (Figure 2.4). Sam described China as a peaceful place in the clouds where the gods lived. The only being that was allowed to go between the worlds was a "parrot god" for which he chose the figurine of Isis, unbeknownst to Sam, the Egyptian goddess of child birth and motherhood, and considered the ideal mother and wife.

At this point in the play, Sam turned to me and asked about my newborn son and if he was with his mother at this moment. When I answered that my son was indeed with my wife, we then engaged in a conversation about his mother and sibling. Sam became sad and described the loneliness he feels when his mother is not available to be with him. He stated an understanding that realistically his mother needs to be more available to his sibling, but was able to acknowledge the longing he feels to be with her. This dialogue was the first time Sam was able to discuss his feelings about his mother and sibling's illness without being guarded.

Sam's anger was clearly on the surface, but when he literally tunneled through the destruction and rage, he could access the other emotions of sadness, longing, and loneliness. Sam wanted a place of serenity, but his anger created this world of rage and destruction. By offering a path to another possibility, another part of himself, we were able to journey into a place of genuine and deep experience, the place we needed to go in order to access the healing power within. After this session, Sam's behavior became more authentic in that he was able to exhibit the behaviors that were described by school and his parents – the self-abasing comments and negative self-image. There seemed to be a shift where Sam was able to access a more authentic way of relating and playing. He had the ability to explore more positive ways of interacting with others. By acknowledging his feelings, he was able to move past them and gain more control of his behaviors. Sam needed to find this place deep within himself, and in fact, months later he again created a tunnel, embellishing the opening with a smooth layer of sparkly glitter. When I asked him to describe the content of the tunnel, he smiled and simply said, "Peace."

Dynamic play therapy is an effective technique to engage in more in-depth psychotherapy with children because of their ability to spontaneously engage in a dialogue with their unconscious. Adults, however, are difficult to engage in this type of spontaneous treatment as we are often caught up in our ego defenses, which guard us from experiencing vulnerability. Using the imagination assists a process of healing, as it leads to a pathway to the unconscious. Like dreams, it can engage a dialogue and symbolic story of what is occurring beneath the surface. This process requires that we open ourselves to freely journey into our inner core.

At night we have dreams. During the day we have our imagination. Both symbolically represent a communication with our unconscious (Johnson 1986). Focusing our awareness on the symbols that come from our imagination is a significant resource to developing a life that is more wholly understood. Carl Jung integrated this theory in his practice by using a technique he called Active Imagination, in which he guided his patients into a type of meditative state and asked them to communicate with the spontaneous images that emerged from their imagination. Before its introduction to modern times by Jung, this process was used throughout ancient history, as it was understood even then that man had a seamless relationship with the unconscious. Whether recognizing the forces of the gods or the signs and omens from native witch doctors and shamans, man has allowed himself to be guided by these images.

I have found that utilizing Jung's approach of Active Imagination has allowed my adult clients to engage with the images from their unconscious. Derek is a 24-year-old client who is in the early stages of committing to a religious order. Our sessions focused on his varying desire to fully commit to this way of life while weighing his secular struggles with rebellious behavior, substance use, and sex. Derek questioned whether his commitment would be false, as he was used to numbing his true feelings with reckless behavior. I started to incorporate Active Imagination into our sessions while attempting to access these aspects of himself that he had closed off. During one session, Derek described a giant wall that provided a division between a large field on one side and a cave on the other. During the next several sessions, he conjured the image of an elfin figure that lived in the cave. Derek would engage in a dialogue with the elf in order to seek answers from his unconscious.

Over the course of our therapy together, Derek came to understand that it was more valuable to unearth and reconcile these hidden feelings than to numb and avoid them. Together, we explored the image of the cave as a pathway to his inner world.

He used the elfin figure as a messenger between his unconscious and conscious thoughts, asking it unanswered questions about the inaccessible and cut-off feelings he began to realize were at the source of his confusion. When asking the elf about this confusion, the elf emerged from the cave bringing a woman to explain that while Derek was holding on to the anger from his childhood, he was ignoring the immense love that has continually been present in his family. With this answer, Derek was able to release the anger and on some level grieve the lost time he had spent holding on to it. I encouraged him, outside of our sessions, to journey to this cave, this portal to the unconscious, where instead of blocking his expression with maladaptive behaviors, he can engage with the process that is calling him to seek answers and deepen his relationship to his Self.

D.W. Winnicott (1971) wrote, "It is in playing and only in playing that the individual child or adult is able to be creative and to use the whole personality, and it is only in being creative that the individual discovers the Self" (p.25). Whether working with children or adults, the craft of psychotherapy is a unique way in which we assist the process of communicating with our client's inner world. The images that arise from imaginative play are important symbols from the unconscious that guide psychotherapy. Much like an archeological site, the act of digging deep with our clients and unearthing hidden secrets is an intricate, slow, deliberate process, that when rushed, can lead to damage. Like the message in "The Portal," it is not about a quick fix when we consider treatment and outcome.

With the case examples presented, it seems important to have a guide to make the journey for us, or along with us, into our tunnels and caves. Matthew's Portal has a guardian, Sam's tunnel is only passable by a mother goddess, Peter relied on me to join him on the expedition, and Derek's elf makes it possible for him to face the journey from the safety of the mouth of the tunnel, without having to submerge into the dark unknown alone. Unconsciously, there is an understanding that our tunnels contain great and sometimes overwhelming knowledge, therefore we need to respect this sacred space of our clients.

This archetypal use of tunnel and caves in my work has provided a way for me to witness and respect the process of individuation especially in children. However, it is not the structure of the tunnel, rather the void that it provides, where transformation occurs. We must therefore offer the appropriate holding environment to support and encourage creative imagination, so as to assist in the process of envisioning possibility, helping to bring the unseen to the surface, and to emerge successfully out of the tunnel.

To my wife and companion Meg Rodier, who helped me unearth this chapter from my depths.

References

Johnson, R.A. (1986) *Inner Work: Using Dreams and Active Imagination for Personal Growth.* New York, NY: Harper Collins.

Neumann, E. (1973) *The Child* (R. Manheim Trans.) Boston, MA: Shambhala Publications, Inc.

Sobel, D. (1993) *Children's Special Places: Exploring the Role of Forts, Dens, and Bush Houses in Middle Childhood.* Tucson, AZ: Zephyr Press.

Winnicott, D.W. (1971) *Playing and Reality.* New York, NY: Routledge.

CHAPTER THREE

The Keys to the World

Revolution and Epiphany in Deep Sand

Julie Lyon Rose

Five-year-old T. finished a series of stories, using a deep sandbox over several sessions, by burying an old bunch of keys. Before he left he dug them out again, handed them to me and said "these are the keys to the world."

First, a few roots. I experience word roots as ancient doorways to understanding, and helpful clues. A linguistic tug on a word unearths the often unseen way in which its meaning can be physically expressed.

The word "poetry" comes from the Greek root to create, pile up, build; "dream" from the Saxon for joy, mirth, music; "revolution", to turn or roll, wallow, with "wellspring" sharing the same root; "play", to engage oneself, to pledge, "epiphany" to shine. These roots seem particularly appropriate to the use of deep sand in therapy, both literally and symbolically. They also support my experience of play, as an irreducible and completely necessary state of being. Play encompasses poetry as a creative dive towards the core of self and of the world. Play encompasses dream as the unbounded emergence from that personal and collective core. Revolution emerges as joyful piling and building draw the player into a productive and rolling wallow. Epiphany describes the numinous and luminous quality that fills the room when a child discovers both a physical and symbolic revolution in the sand.

Often a child will come to play more or less disembodied due to trauma or difficult physical growth patterns. He may be in a kind of dream, with a shaky or unbounded sense of self, and/or in a rigid poetic state, his creativity too tightly held. Disconnected, he does not seem to fully know or trust his own body, his own feet. Dream and poetry need to be integrated, brought to ground, fully claimed and internalized. This is where the revolution inherent in play can heal, with the always awe-inspiring turn into full embodiment, the healing wallow, the return to the wellspring.

In play, revolution is storytelling seeded in dream, emerging as poetry. Deep sand invites the digging, piling, stamping, jumping, pounding, stirring, shaping, spilling, and other wild dancing ways of play that life force follows in order to descend through dream and poetry into full embodiment.

The therapist, as attendant, by being fully present in the play space and willing to join in the dream and the poetry of the play, is a reassuring catalyst for the child's descent. Joining in involves listening, watching, and wondering. In my experience, if the therapist interprets what's emerging in an analytical way during play, she is no longer present and the playing child senses the loss right away of the safety, of whole-hearted companionship. This can block the flow of play. The therapist needs to be in a state of wonder so that when the impulse to understand rises up it becomes wondering.

T., presenter of the keys to the world, came to therapy when he was four years old. He was plagued by serious asthma, had a mild speech disorder, and seemed awkward and regressed in the way he moved, almost as if he were walking in a dream. His family life was secure with a loving mother and father in the home but his asthma had precipitated a few scary trips to the emergency room. He experienced separation anxiety, sometimes panicky before school and would often say he was lonely. From the beginning of our play together, he was a coherent and articulate storyteller, with a precocious vocabulary, describing action and intention as it unfolded.

I will tell the stories as T. told them, in the present tense and frequently with his use of words.

T.'s Stories

First session

There's a river that flows in a circle. Fishing boats line up on the river. There's a house in the middle of the circle where a man lives. A space shuttle is parked nearby. An old yellow car, missing one wheel, is partly buried so the man has to go places in the space shuttle. Also on the island is a lighthouse. A cowboy lives in the lighthouse tower and firemen live in the small attached house. They have two fire trucks and a hydrant. Outside of the circle of the river is a small house where a construction man lives. He has a tractor and two bulldozers.

Across the way, on the other side of the circle are two castles, side by side. A giant fly lives in them. A supersnake comes and eats the fly. It also takes a bite out of a fireman who dies and is buried by the lighthouse. Then all the other snakes, whose home extended to the bottom of the ocean, came to live with the supersnake. They pile on top of and wind around the castles.

A bad guy arrives inside the circle and quickly buries all the houses, including the lighthouse, all the people, the space shuttle and the fire trucks. The island has become a bare mountain. The construction man comes with a bulldozer and digs them out.

In the end, two fish and a good shark, who eats bad people, live in the river which is also an ocean. They are separated by the boats but can dive deep underneath to find each other.

At this point, as the unexpected erupts, T. speaks more loudly and with gusto. His telling is interspersed with moving the sand, finding and placing objects, and heavy, concentrated breathing which increases as more chaos then enters the story. As the unexpected erupts, T. speaks with increasing gusto and volume. Humor and wonder fill his face.

Several following sessions

The story repeats with only slight variations.

There must be a road! The road runs through the center of the land, dividing it in half. It is made of colorful blocks, red, green, blue, yellow, purple. A small house is on one side, often on fire. There are many orange emergency cones and "slow – accident" signs. There is traffic on the road that spills into the danger zones on either side and is directed by policemen and the signs. There is a bad guy, who sometimes rides a motorcycle and seems always to be escaping on the opposite side of the road from the burning house. The castle is his home. It doesn't burn. Finally the road is placed across the land on a diagonal.

Final session

T. comes in looking fierce. Up until now he has come in with a soft, dreamy expression and a doddery way of moving which has been lessening over time. In previous sessions, he has started by placing things very carefully in the sand. This time, he grabs a big, heavy rubber mallet and swings hard making two generous holes in the sand.

> The holes are entrances to an underground highway. An ambulance is going in one end and coming out the other. Strange objects fall into the land. An enormous blue hand as well as blue and purple balls with tentacles. I am ordered to set up a village. A castle flies in and lands upside down nearby. There was a cave for a dragon underneath it but now the dragon has flown. The village is toppled.
>
> Then a large pirate ship arrives and anchors. The anchor rope stretches in a diagonal across the whole land. Two birds are planted upside down and a rainbow felt ball balanced on top of them. A while later, a shell is plunked on top of the ball. That's the home. Marbles and crystals are scattered over the whole land. Then the colorful road is laid down, coming in over the edge, on the end opposite the pirate ship. A police van drives along it heading for the paths that go down to the underground world. They take an umbrella down because they're vacationing underground. Far away in the other side is a bad guy on a motorcycle.
>
> Now a maze and a golden tablet are buried with a bunch of keys near the upside down castle. Then a lot of stuff is tossed into the world. Baby rattles, ping-pong ball, an earth ball, a broken transformer (space ship), fake cat vomit. After standing for a moment, T. unearths the keys and hands them to me, "the keys to the world."

Revolution filled the room!

After each sand story, T. had pounded or chopped clay and hit a big pad with a foam bat, making a very loud sound. This time, he cut a huge island of clay into tiny pieces very quickly and threw them in the bowl of water for washing hands saying "It feels like poop!" He then tossed the pad in another box of very wet sand and stuffed a can of markers underneath it. I felt that he needed to feel the strength and freshness of this revolution in his body. I think he would have liked to wreck the room but it was time to go. He swaggered out, looking tall and awake, his old garments of overflowing dreams and careful poetry in shreds, making room for the sacred fool, the hero, the more fully embodied boy.

T. didn't come back to the playroom for about five months. He was doing fine going off to school and his asthma was much milder. He came back after a serious bout of asthma and some subsequent return of separation anxiety.

Two sessions

> The road is a circle carved in the sand, fluid and shifting. A house burns, the fire is put out and the ashes cleaned up with a bulldozer. The bad guy comes to steal all the gold but the police catch him. They shout "you are surrounded" and he says "I don't want to go with you."
>
> There is a round road with a house on one side and a castle, the fire station, on the other side. The house is burning and all the rescue vehicles surround it: police cars, fire trucks, rescue helicopter, ambulances, also firemen, emergency stop lights and orange cones. The sirens are loud. [T. makes ear splitting siren sounds. He never did this in any of his previous sessions. The session before this one, he asked me to write the whooo, whooos and he taped them on the side of the sandbox.] The fire is out, a bulldozer clears away the burnt house, another bulldozer clears the ashes leaving a hollow where a digger makes a deep trench. All the rescue vehicles go into the trench.
>
> Now the castle, the fire station, is burning so all the rescue vehicles come out of the trench and put out the fire. Then a big wheel comes and smashes and smashes the burnt firehouse to collapse it down because it is weak and squishy. A big turtle comes and accompanies the ambulance to the hospital that is outside of the sandbox. It is big and has a garage extension.

These two sessions felt very different to me from T.'s earlier sessions. His movements and speech were heartier and more direct and he seemed to be dealing with the reality and logistics surrounding his asthma. In his earlier sessions I felt he was mapping his body, his nervous system, and respiratory system in the sand in an ultimately successful attempt to fully inhabit himself. After he presented the keys to the world to me, I felt he was able to see his asthma as a problem to be solved rather than being overwhelmed by the confusion and fear of blocked breathing, the emergency treatment and the alarm of the people around him.

There are many ways to interpret T.'s play or any child's play. For me, if I've been successfully present during a play session, then useful understanding comes easily afterwards. Useful understanding opens up helpful communication with, and support for, parents and caregivers and subtly changes the atmosphere in the next session. The child feels understood.

A final thought. If you deny the mystery inherent in communication through play, then you constrict room for breathing and growing and thus for liberation through wholeness. I believe any understanding of play needs to come with open arms, open hands, open face, open heart, and open mind, allowing for a full embrace of the indescribable and the mysterious.

CHAPTER FOUR

Behold the Treasure and the Swamp!

Digging, Delving, Poking, Pounding, and Getting to the Bottom of Things

Michelle Rhodes

Figure 4.1: Three Islands and a Swamp

Introduction

In this chapter I shall explore the changing play imagery of an eight-year-old boy I shall call Pete. He was the middle son from a stable, upwardly mobile family residing in a small city. Pete presented with an Asperger's-like combination of characteristics (McPartland *et al.* 2014). Developmentally out of balance, Pete was way ahead in his verbal skills but he lagged behind age peers in motor and social skills. In addition, he had fears. His parents reported that Pete's fears often led to demands and meltdowns that ended up interfering with family activities and sleep. Helium balloons were a particular source of dread for Pete, ruining many a birthday celebration, as he feared they would get loose, float away and never be seen again. It wasn't just the loss of a balloon that concerned him. It was that it detached and disappeared.

I saw Pete for a total of eight months, during which time he celebrated his ninth birthday.

Case Study: The sessions with Pete

Pete spends most of every session using the sand tray. His narrative seems pressured to continue for as long as there is sand, water, miniatures and time. Much of his play involves flooding the tray with water, though for a couple of sessions he sculpts clay.

Words fail me as I revisit video recordings of sessions with Pete. There is so much happening, the play is so rich, the narrative so complex, the three dimensionality of it, the movement, the sounds of the materials and the miniatures, the visual impact all overwhelm my verbal capacity. I wonder how it can ever be possible to convey this in a meaningful way. Accuracy is out of the question – still photographs are mere maps.

My best hope for conveying the transformative process of Pete's play is to start this piece of writing as if it were a film, with no more explanation, in medias res, midstream. So here goes.

We see the chubby hands of a boy, miniatures, a sand tray. We hear his child-voice narrating at a good clip and the wet sand gobs plop plop plop plopping into the water. 'Am I da puhson who probly used the mos' wadr in dis…? Maybe dey …not so much water, …stream maybe.' His speech is slurred and soft around the edges, but if we listen carefully we can understand him most of the time. We sense the presence of an observer, and we hear her following and facilitating the play, mirroring, asking questions and voicing exclamations of surprise, glee, grunt-words, mm's, ah's and oh's. It's a duet. Her part is the *continuo* – his, the *recitative*.

He enters fully into his play, building an island by dropping gobs of wet sand. He repeats the scooping and plopping. He sighs, becomes calm. His first sand tray includes the swordswoman, rarely used by boys. She becomes a regular character in his stories. Islands also become fixtures, to the extent anything is fixed. The figures are in the water, covered up with sand, pulled out, covered up again. He rescues them from their stuck state, re-embeds them, and rescues them again. At the end all of them get washed to sea.

Figure 4.2: Left to Right: Swordswoman, Biker Boar with Electric Robot on His Back, Statue of Boy with Snake Goddess above and behind Him.

Pete is here for his fourth visit. He creates a scene in the wet sand. There is a bed with two pillows and a lace coverlet, rocking chair, fireplace, standing mirror, couch, bathtub, toilet, sink, refrigerator, and table with straight back chairs.

He adds a cash register, first aid kit, canon, statue of a boy, dinosaur skeleton, gravestone, and small piece of fence. The dinosaur skeleton is half buried in wet sand, near the gravestone, fence, and canon. There has been some kind of invasion. Table and chairs are overturned, the statue is sprawled on the fireplace. Wet sand has rained down and is on the furnishings, giving a decidedly uncared-for look to the place.

The cash register is in the middle of the scene. From where Pete stands, the bed is at upper right. Gravestone, canon, and dinosaur skeleton are at far left. Bathroom things are in the upper midsection. The full-length mirror is in front of the refrigerator in the bottom left. There are half-buried shovels as well. Someone has been digging in search of something. Near the gravestone, in the backyard area, is an old-fashioned well pump. Given how much water gets poured into his scenes, we might need to pump some out! Or perhaps the pump is there to draw water up from a deeper place. Water, in any case, has come to be an essential material for Pete's play. He explains his scene:

> It's an abandoned house. The people have died of old age. There were only two people, see, two pillows on the bed. [He points, touching each pillow.] Only two people. No children. The old people died a long time ago. Lots of people have been digging around since then looking for treasure. The old people were really rich. They also had pets that died, and that gravestone out there is where they were buried.

He has already poured some additional water on the damp sand. He adds blue glass pebble gems and plastic crystal diamonds which are deposited next to the cash register. As the action picks up momentum he adds things in groups – fistfuls of tiny ninjas, little metal knights in armor, and green plastic army figures. All the furniture is by this time topsy-turvy. Nothing is left standing. The bathtub is filled with objects and figures, embedded in a tightly packed ball of sand. The large skeleton has a lapful of green army figures. Half a dozen pirates arrive next in a sailboat. A large canon is added, and another skeleton.

The treasure hunters find some beer and a hero sandwich. As Pete presses the gems and diamonds into the sand he tells me the treasure is 'bedded (embedded) because it is so heavy. He will use this term often over many sessions to come.

By the time we get close to the end of the session, the scene is approaching maximum holding capacity. He has been adding water by the cupful. The sand is quite sloppy and wet, and the tray is very crowded. He tells me he needs still more water, and at first uses a ladle to pour water over the tub and free its contents. He adds more and more water, eventually dumping the entire water bucket he had filled. Where there was sloppy wet sand, now there is deep water over its surface. He doesn't name this body of water but I will refer to it as a swamp, because it seems a stagnant place. So much gets stuck there. Pete digs around in this swamp bottom like someone digging for clams, and finding objects, rinses them in the swamp water and examines them one by one. This appears to be a necessary cleansing. He washes and examines what he has removed from inside of himself, making it conscious. Meanwhile he talks about ordinary reality, asking me how many kids come here, guessing maybe six, and adds, "counting me." He is calm and relaxed. We are having a conversation. He wants to know exactly. I add that grownups come too, which is a surprise to him. Reality can be strange.

Pete hovers between the real and the fantasy worlds. He wants to be able to fly away. He is not sure if monsters or perhaps which monsters are real, and asks my opinion. He remembers detailed information from real science and from fantasy. Once he has stored the information in his memory, fact and fiction are no longer kept in separate categories.

Mentally Pete inhabits a science fiction world in which if he thinks something hard enough and sees it in his mind clearly and with enough detail it becomes real, or he can make it real, or he can make make-believe real. I experience a flash of happy anticipation that he will someday use this gift to create terrific fiction, yet I am aware that this gift of imagination comes at a price. What if he imagines he is the balloon and it floats away? What if he imagines his parents dying? What if he imagines he disintegrates? On the other hand, in spite of his deep commitment to the fantasy world, he is oriented to reality. He can interrupt the most complicated fantasy sand-story with tidbits of reality. Hearing his mother's arrival, he looks up at me and asks if it is time to go. I assure him that we still have time. He comments that she's early, because last time she was late so I asked her to come early this time. He plays on, digging in the wet sand, and finding the mirror, wipes the sand off, commenting that it got all sandy. Then he lifts up the large skeleton and he is back in his story, telling me that the skeleton can easily survive, that actually skeletons can't die because they're already dead, and it might bother the skeleton to have his head in the sand but it wouldn't kill him because he can't even breathe. Reality and fantasy are interwoven. This is play. Or is it more real than make-believe for him?

Examining the tiny plastic champagne bottle he is just fishing out from the depths, he asks if there was ever anything in it, commenting that it looks like a real beer bottle, and he thought maybe it was a teensy teensy teensy teensy teensy weensy real one. Pete then invites me into a discussion of exactly how much beer the teensy weensy bottle could actually hold, if it could or ever did really contain any beer, and he decides quite logically and correctly that it would hold less than an ounce. This shift from the imaginary to the real sets Pete apart from a child who is clearly in play mode and whose narrative might go from teensy teensy weensy real beer bottle to teensy teensy weensy real people or ninjas or even mice or insects or birds who would enjoy the beer. Abandoning play mode Pete goes in the opposite direction, to science and spatial figuring, and compares the possible capacity of the miniature bottle to how many ounces are in a soda bottle, in a liter, and tells how much he drank at a party, until his stomach hurt, his brain was tingling, and it felt like his veins would break. As we discuss his and the bottle's capacity for holding fizzy beverages I have a flash of worry that I am in the presence of a future alcoholic, but my attention is brought back to the present by his hands, which are busy in the water again. He has pushed the overturned items and drowned figures away from him and is dragging his fingers through the sand slurry, pouring wet gobs from hand to hand. Rinse. Repeat. I drift into reverie[1] as I gaze at Pete's scene, I see the large skeleton lying prone on the box that was the old couple's bed, his upper body hanging over the edge of the box, and I think perhaps he is seeking his reflection in the now calm waters. What is he thinking? "Oh, I'm a skeleton. Look at that. I must be dead." At the far end of the sand tray, next to the half submerged refrigerator, a lone pirate, a soggy book and a small canon are drying out in the sailboat. I imagine the sun beating down. Deep in

---

1   As described by Patrick Casement (1991 p. 37) reverie is a term used by Wilfred Bion (1962, 1963, 1965) to describe the function of a mother's capacity to both contain her infant's unbearable emotional states and to nurture the infant's capacity to digest experience, in other words, to think, or to use a more contemporary neologism, to mentalize (Fonagy *et al.* 2002). Casement quotes Bion's 1962 book *Learning from Experience* as follows: "There is thus a need, for the baby – that is, for its mental growth and maturation – for a detour through the Other."

the swamp, drowned soldiers. On the shore, a ransacked household, and abandoned treasure. Thus ends today's episode.

A week later Pete is back. He goes immediately to the cardboard bricks, which he stacks as high as he can until they fall over. Then he floods the sand tray and brings in the human skeletons, dinosaur skeleton, canons, pirates, knights in armor, tiny ninjas, and two special pebbles that represent the team flags. The narrated story is simple, there are two teams, and whoever has the flags has the advantage. Pete does not seem invested in the story today. There doesn't appear to be a battle going on, but he does say the ninjas are preparing for their second and ultimate attack on the big skeleton. In a trance-like state, he reaches again and again into the water, pulling things out, half-heartedly looking for the flag-pebbles, but he finds several tiny ninjas instead and shows me how they attack the large skeleton. They fill up the skeleton's ribcage until it seems it would burst. I am reminded of the feeling Pete describes having after he drank too much soda. When the last ninja is thrust forcefully up into the ribcage cavity, the thrusting has a phallic quality to it, unlike his typical moves in which figures attack with mouths, or simply bump into each other. The thrusting nearly forces some of the ninjas out at the neck. End of attack. The ninjas are dumped out of the rib cavity and Pete gets quiet. He digs in the wet sand a little, scoops some up, lets it plop back into the water. After noting that lots of things are bedded in the sand (stuck and barely visible), he pushes and packs as much sand as he can, along with various pirates and a few miscellaneous ninjas, onto the big skeleton. Again in a dreamy state, he pushes at the sand slowly, enjoying the sensual quality of the sand and water.

Then, as if he has suddenly awakened, remembering that he was burying the large skeleton he becomes energized and quickly completes the burial. Then, without clear plot point for this next move but with very clear intention and dynamic action, he frees the large skeleton, shoves him into the corner, and pushes sand onto him, immobilizing him for a second time.

At this point Pete says he is going to make a dam. Though time is up, the concept has been introduced. It is the beginning of Pete's bringing structure into contact with chaos.

Figure 4.3: Two-headed Dragon

Working with clay

Pete decides to explore the clay studio and for two sessions is engaged in making a dragon. After vigorously pounding the clay to get it ready, we sit down together at the clay table. He is fascinated by the slip, a slurry of clay and water used to join pieces of clay together; a wing onto a dragon body, or a head onto a neck, for example. He wants to paint with the slip, but I guide his attention to the rather challenging task of dragon construction. He starts with the idea of a dragon from a book he has read, but quickly changes his mind and just follows the flow of his imagination. Looking around and noticing sculptures and pottery on the shelves, including a dragon or two, he asks again how many other kids I see.

I provide technical assistance while Pete provides creative genius and his own personal touch. By the end of two sessions the dragon is looking good. Pete has completed and joined together two heads, necks, a body, wings, spikes, and a tail. Cleaning up at the sink, he becomes so intrigued by the natural sponges it is hard to get him out the door.

Why, in such a child-guided play therapy/art therapy context, do I frustrate Pete's desire to mess around with the slip? I do this for a couple of reasons. I want to see what happens when he doesn't get to do what he initially wants. I want to see what it is like to collaborate with him, and I want to see if he can manage the combination of chaos and structure, infinite possibility, and limitation that is such a big part of working with clay. Unlike sand, clay is something in which you leave your mark and it can become permanent. But until the moment you stop affecting it, it is so changeable that a tiny twitch of a finger can totally alter the expression of a face, figure or abstract form. I throw my weight on the side of structure to see if Pete will go with it. I also think that if he can stay with the project he will be very proud of the dragon we can collaborate in making and would have the opportunity to enjoy a real, rather than a fantasized, triumph. Another value of staying focused on the creative task is that in working together we build our relationship more than when I am *continuo* accompaniment to his *recitative*. In this process there is more opportunity for him to ask for and receive help, and for me to anticipate his needs and respond to his requests, all in the service of enhancing his real self in the physical and interactional world and helping him to feel more at ease. I wonder if the dragon can contain and symbolically direct Pete's aggression so he can experience its positive energy. Dragon fire has directionality, and a dragon in flight can see the big picture. The dragon, a cave dweller with wings, can symbolize a *syzygy*,[2] the union of opposites – earth and sky, darkness and light.

Increasingly, pairs of opposites appear in Pete's sandplay. In the next few weeks he begins to use both the wet and the dry sand trays. He explores the soft texture and flowing quality of the dry sand, deciding that it looks and smells like flour. He brings the large wooden castle and ordinary farm animals into his story, balancing this ordinariness with musings about reality and fantasy, saying "I wish I could be a toy." And "I want to be a ninja when I grow up, because I'm sneaky and I have swords."

From this point on Pete's play regularly includes both the wet and the dry sand. At one point in his play he sets up an orderly scene in the dry sand. Figures from the flooded wet sand come over to the dry area to attack. When the battle is going full tilt the skeleton army is called in to fight a gigantic snake. Disorder threatens to take over the dry sand tray, but for full chaos the figures need to return to the swamp

---

2   Jung used the term *syzygy* to refer to the co-existence and co-functioning of opposites. They do not blend, but are linked, as the cerebral Apollonian masculine and the chthonic Dionysian feminine might be. See Claire Douglas's chapter "The historical context of analytical psychology" Chapter 1 p.23 in Young-Eisendrath, P., and Dawson, T. *The Cambridge Companion to Jung* (1997).

where much exciting action ensues. When it comes to an end, ninjas, dinosaurs, skeletons, food, treasure, and potent alcoholic drinks are gathered into a mound of packed sand where they remain, embedded. Chaos has been unleashed, recaptured and contained. Structure has been re-established. Pete stands by and surveys the final scene with satisfaction.

Freedom and power

It is Pete's fourteenth session. The dragon sculpture has exploded in the kiln. I have reassembled it in the dry sand with the sand supporting the parts. It doesn't look too bad and to my surprise Pete is not at all upset, even though he had worked hard making it. If it did indeed contain his aggression, wouldn't it be proper for it to explode in the kiln? For Pete, the explosion trumps the loss of the sculpture. Besides, he can see that I have the (magical?) power to make it whole again.

I wonder to myself if Pete's nonchalance also indicates something about Pete's experience of continuity, constancy, trust, and attachment. While at times he can't let go, at other times he seems remarkably detached. For him the explosion makes the piece special – magical and powerful. He also feels honored to be the one whose piece exploded when I tell him this is a rarity that happens once every five years. I explain how the piece can be mended. He agrees to let me do it and turns to the sand, playing as I mend. When I am finished, Pete says he likes how the dragon looks scarred and bloody from battle. He does not want to cover up the mending with paint. How marvelous! He (Pete? The Dragon?) has exploded, and I have put him back together again. We didn't even need all-the-king's-horses and men.

Pete creates three mounds in the wet sand and names them "Snake Mountain", "Dinosaur Mountain" and "Ninja Mountain." He sets up a complex scene using many familiar elements and figures: deep water, the miniature bottles, the statue of the boy, blue glass pebble gems, the hero sandwich, pirates, and ninjas. The Statue of Liberty and Electric Robot make their first appearance. The swordswoman is back in after a long absence. Pirate booty is hidden, uncovered and fought over, creating the usual mayhem. In the end, the mountains nearly leveled, a pigeon swoops out of the sky and rescuing the Statue of Liberty out of the swamp, stands her up on a little pile of sand. Electric Robot's head, having been knocked off, hops across the wet sand to his robot body, and says "stupid body!" as it is snapped back into place. I make note of the head reuniting with the body and the proximity of the rescued Statue of Liberty. Is there a connection? Perhaps Pete is discovering a new ease and freedom as his head and body make a good connection.

Bringing opposites together

With this next session a new chapter of play begins. In dry sand, the table and book have returned from that scene long ago where the old couple had died. The Statue of Liberty, a newcomer as of last session, has returned and stands at the front and center of the dry sand, overlooking the wet, which has been flooded as usual. There are several caches, each with its protection. Cannon protects fruit and vegetables, cave and volcano hold glass gems, diamonds are hidden under the bridge. Eggs are near the cave, half hidden behind it. Two big milk bottles in their carrier are at the rear center. The sailboat is also present on dry sand. All face toward the wet sand tray. Pete adds the snake goddess for the first time today. She will remain a presence in many future episodes.

By the end of this session all the figures have disappeared beneath the wet sand. The boat remains in the dry sand, with the animal skull next to it to show just how devoid of water this scene is, how opposite from the swamp.

Two sessions later there are farm animals again in the dry sand, along with vegetables, skeletons, a life boat, the Bible, milk bottles, and two small snakes. A cactus and the animal skull demonstrate how dry this scene is. There is a new plot element. A powerful female, a witch or the swordswoman, must be buried alive, immobilized but not quite killed off. Like many parts of his psyche undergoing change, she needs to be acted upon repeatedly, and so she is killed, almost but not completely, so she can be killed again, and again, and again. Giving something up (killing it off) can take multiple attempts.

Violence happens in the wet sand tray, where among three familiar islands we find the pirates in the sailboat, and many other figures including a large snake, dinosaur skeleton, green plastic soldiers, electric robot, and the sometimes dead swordswoman. Birds have multiplied and become an important part of the action, flying from island to island, transferring and protecting wealth and goods. To keep the witch immobilized, she is stuffed head first into a basket, then sand is packed around her. To make absolutely sure she stays put, other things are piled on top: the statue of the boy, a dead horse, and other objects. In the end, there is no person or animal left in the dry sand. The warring groups have traded locations and intermingled. All structures and categories have disintegrated into chaos. All the figures are under water. Pete rains wet sand down onto the watery scene and the session ends. The rain of wet sand seems to function like a theater curtain, marking the end of an episode.

Alignment and symmetry

The following week a new figure becomes central. He is a very tough
male, Biker Boar, complete with leather pants, goggles and chain. What
is astonishing, though, is not only that Biker Boar is seated on a single
elevated plain that stretches all the way across the tub of wet sand,
and not that he gazes across from there to the dry sand, what is
most astonishing is Pete's choice of some beautiful, delicate, feminine
symbols laid in a line on the land that slopes down from Biker Boar
to the water.

Figure 4.4: The Goddess Aligned

There is a stork, a single blue glass gem, a fertility goddess, and a hero
sandwich. Over in the dry sand, the castle is central, and the drama
around it involves medieval characters. There is a royal family with
their accumulated wealth and their entourage. This wealth is not so
haphazard as some buried treasure an old couple left behind when
they died. This wealth is for the living. It is carefully stowed in the castle
tower, along with a supply of excellent foods, protected by cannons
and knights in armor. On the wet side Biker Boar has the pirates and
the milk to his far right, a pile of ninjas and the eggs to his far left, and
two guardian birds by his feet. All is balanced and even. Behind Biker
Boar, a round mirror creates a nimbus, showing just how powerful and

special Biker Boar is. And he has wealth — two large symmetrically placed balls of money. Some of the figures and objects remain in their original places. Pete uses only a limited amount of water this time. There is no flood.

Before the episode ends, though, everyone is killed by electrocution, zapped by the robot. He shoots electricity at the mirror, where it is reflected back and destroys every living thing. Pete rinses his hands in the wet tray, as always, and declares, "That's the end. This is the first time I actually finished!"

In future sessions Biker Boar continues to play a central role. Pete has made the Boar a clay throne. It does not explode when fired, but becomes solid and will survive floods, providing solid ground for the most powerful surviving figures. Buried treasure, food, and embedded stuckness no longer dominate Pete's stories. Instead he incorporates more structural elements: castle, walls, the throne, and a high wooden arch. Electricity becomes the primary destructive force.

Figure 4.5: Monster Drawing: Shadow Ninja

The snake goddess appears every week now, energetically flinging her boomerangs/snakes, at times occupying the throne in place of the Boar. In one of Pete's final scenes the boy statue comes to life, and the electric robot is given a place of honor atop the castle tower.

Initial clinical picture

Pete's parents initially brought him for play therapy because his behavior was interfering with normal family life. He had been given a diagnosis of social anxiety disorder by a developmental pediatrician several years before. His verbal skills were several years above grade level but his motor skills lagged far behind, which may explain why, although he had an impressive vocabulary, his words were not clearly articulated.

Pete was often frightened at night and would wake his parents for comfort. They reported, and he confirmed, that he was very anxious around helium balloons, fearing that they would escape. He was afraid other toys would blow away.

There were a host of neurological signs that suggested something other than a diagnosis of social anxiety disorder. He engaged in repetitive actions like rubbing his face, making a "tsk" sound and a repetitive throat-clearing noise. He recited facts without regard for his listener's interest. He needed to make things even. He was bothered by certain textures, would wear only soft clothing. Recently he had been gaining weight, and would only eat fatty foods, soda, and sweets.

Core issues

While it is a human struggle to find balance between the forces of order and chaos, it is a core issue for those such as Pete whose neurological wiring makes them particularly vulnerable to obsessive-compulsive behaviors. People with such wiring manage anxiety, worry, and stress by such Apollonian approaches as cleaning, counting, controlling, measuring, intellectualizing, and being generally rigid and in control of themselves and others, or alternatively taking a Dionysian approach and hoarding, bingeing, drinking and drugging, focusing on excrement, being messy, and being out of control.[3] Often there is a seesawing from one extreme to the other.

In Pete's play we see him gradually bring the Dionysian feminine chthonic into line uniting it with the Apollonian fleshless electric masculine. In the end, after Electric Robot does everyone in, the Sculpture Boy is liberated from his frozen state.

Shadow Ninja, the subject of Pete's initial monster drawing, can release lethal electric currents from its hands like Electric Robot. It is a reference to a commercial monster, not one that Pete invented, but it beautifully presages the robotic hero of his story, who ultimately brings the boy back to life.

Ending

When I meet with Pete's parents a month after Biker Boar, Snake Goddess and Electric Robot become active in Pete's play, they report that although Pete has had one full meltdown during the winter holidays, there has also been much progress. Pete has decided to give up his blankie, making do with just a little piece of it. He is reflecting on how his actions affect others, and apologizes in a heartfelt way when he has hurt someone's feelings. The phobia about helium balloons is gone. He is able to share, and he is no longer obsessed with soda.

Symbolism and the therapist's mind

There are many ways therapists can work with the deep imagery a patient presents. We can be guided by Jungian archetypes, Freudian drive theory, or any number of culturally diverse systems. We can take a phenomenological approach, attempting to see and describe the image itself in detail. We can engage in reverie, a kind of parallel dream process, or we can be very disciplined and rely only on

---

3   "The quarrel between Apollo and Dionysus is the quarrel between the higher cortex and the older limbic and reptilian brains" (Paglia 1990, p.96). When these two opposing forces are harnessed together and synchronized, rather that competing for control of the psyche, a tremendous amount of creative energy becomes available.

specific information coming from the patient, with no associations from the therapist.[4]

Regardless of the approach taken, there is no way of knowing exactly what any image really means inside of Pete's psyche. I cannot tell him or his parents, or you the reader, what it all means. It was my experience that my own observations and reverie helped me to be attuned to Pete's process and so I share these musings to help the reader better understand how I work.

What I see from overview-in-hindsight of the work with Pete is a series of episodes that are linked. There appears to be a looping linearity. In the end there is a balance of imagery and a coming together of opposites, but that only provides a starting point for another disintegration to take place.

Stages represented in Pete's story

The stages were:

1. death and relinquishing of the baby self that was merged with the mother

2. giving up the breast and the fantasy of omnipotence

3. disintegration of existing self-concepts

4. experiencing chaos

5. facing the terror of disintegration

6. maintaining a sense of self worth in the face of disintegration

7. killing off resistance to change

8. discovering opposites

---

4   Kaufman (2009) emphasizes looking to the patients' material for instruction on how to proceed with the therapy, and states "the ego may not know, but the psyche knows" (p.13). He speaks of translating rather than interpreting an image – translating, that is, from an imaginal to a psychological language, by discerning the image's objective, inherent (archetypal) structure. As such it is a strict phenomenological approach to archetypal work. Rather than interpret the image, Kaufman seeks to understand its message, and to make sure no personal content or interpretation obscures its meaning.

9. creating structure from the ruins

10. sorting out, salvaging and discarding parts of the self

11. allowing the simultaneity of opposites

12. freeing stuck energy.

Images and characters in Pete's play, with my reveries

The following images and characters appeared

- *Animal skull*: Dryness, dry intellect, un-integrated thinking function.

- *Bathroom fixtures*: Attention to and control of bodily functions and cleanliness.

- *Bed with two pillows*: The parental bed, where Pete wants to be but knows it cannot be so.

- *Beer or soda*: Floating away, alcoholism, feeling limits from the inside, feeling real and physical. Pete is both present and floating away when filled to bursting with bubbles. Can he make himself so light that he will float away, or will he burst, exploding like his dragon in the kiln? Bottle as a substitute for the breast.

- *Biker Boar*: Lord of the underworld, he ascends the throne, thus bringing upper and lower realms together. He's energetic, a take-charge kind of guy. Boars are excellent diggers.

- *Birds*: Weave a web among different parts of the self, flying from mountaintop to mountaintop. They are not stuck in the chaotic. Attempting to see the big picture.

- *Bible*: Magical stories.

- *Book*: Pride in his reading skill. Over-dependence on intellectualization.

- *Canons – Large, medium and small*: Pooping machines. They do not seem phallic. Pete is just emerging from his oral/anal stages, where those with OCD often get stuck. The electric rays of his robot may herald the beginning of his phallic stage.

- *Castle and tower.* Offering a greater perspective and a well-organized place to keep supplies and treasure.

- *Cash register.* It is center stage along with treasure in Pete's third sandplay. It lets me know how important it is to Pete to keep track of the value of things. Self-worth. Money = feces. Filthy lucre.[5]

- *Chicken head.* Joy and humor of being only a head, without a "stupid body."

- *Dead couple.* Pete's parents, as they were when he was a baby. Because he is no longer a baby, they no longer exist.

- *Dead pets.* Pete's baby-self, also gone.

- *Dinosaur skeleton.* Old stuff that's still hanging around, but which has lost its flesh and relevance.

- *Dragon.* Transformative magical creature familiar from Pete's reading. Has potential for seeing the big picture. Fearless. Anger can be expressed. Lives in caves and can fly, joining heaven and earth.

- *Electric Robot.* This tiny blue figure is a combination of alien and robot, from a LEGO™ set. Electric Robot, though very small, in the end annihilates everything that had gone before, everything living and dead, old, or threatening. His electricity zaps. Its force is pointed and direct, more refined that a cannon, closer to a spell, but spells deal with the body and are connected to witches, while electrical charges are heady energy like brainwaves and they can stun or kill from a great distance like lightening. They can be invisible as well and so belong in the spirit world a well as the physical. When Pete brings electricity into his story in such a central way, he frees up his own energy. His body and brain receive a jolt and he wakes up out of his stupor.

---

5   Ferenczi (1952, pp.319–331) wrote about the ontogenesis of the interest in money as a progression from interest in feces though increasingly sublimated interests in mud, sand, prettily shaped and colored pebbles, more sophisticated collectibles and finally money.

- *Embedded stuck state*: Pete's entire being, other than his verbal intellect, was stuck and his verbalization sometimes got stuck in the on position.

- *Farm animals*: Ordinary life. Grounded, real, natural. Source of food and energy. Horse-power.

- *Fertility goddess*: The non-threatening integrated feminine as treasure.

- *Flood*: Typically, it represents overwhelming feelings or thoughts. By working repeatedly with this symbol Pete gradually finds a way to transform it from a rough sea with quicksand and mayhem, into a quiet pool.

- *Food*:

  o *Milk bottles*: There are two of them. Breasts.

  o *Big sandwich*: female and/or male genitalia.

  o *Fruits, vegetables, eggs*: healthy way to satisfy hunger. They are of the earth, but not chaotic. Seeds and roots. Contained forms. Potential.

- *Gems and treasure*: Symbols for himself, his value as a person, unaffected by time.

- *Large snake*: Chthonic, oral. Combines masculine and feminine elements, potential for change. Very active transformative symbol.

- *Mountains and islands*: They melt and re-form. Primitive efforts to organize the chaos.

- *Ninjas*: Disorganized energy that needs release. When stuffed inside they cause outbursts and meltdowns.

- *Pirates*: Intentionality. Action guided by thought. They are the captains of the boat.

- *Pump*: Access to greater depths, if needed.

- *Refrigerator*: Source of nourishment, but in cold storage. There are rules about what one can take from there, and rules in general confining Pete's desires. Could the mirror next to it represent the beginning of his capacity to reflect?

- *Sailboat:* Pete's identity on its journey into becoming. It is formed and strengthened each time he intentionally enters or leaves the unruly sea. Sometimes it can rest and enjoy bobbing on the surface, as when Pete enjoys reading or thinking logically.

- *Skeletons large, medium, and small:* Core of the body, but not fleshed out. No muscle. Death. Disintegration.

- *Snake goddess:* More powerful and positive than Swordswoman, she incorporates some of Electric Robot's power to zap, using her snake-boomerangs. She is a counterpart to Motorcycle Boar. She is found in high places, but brings with her and takes charge of the chthonic snake's power.

- *Statue of Boy:* Frozen stuck aliveness. Contains unavailable phallic energy.

- *Statue of Liberty:* Structured feminine symbol of civilization and good government, similar to Snake goddess but without the chthonic element. The grand nurturing goddess, an American Hathor.

- *Stork:* Bringer of babies. Awakening curiosity, concern, confusion about human reproductive functions.

- *Swordswoman:* Representative of the chaotic feminine, attempting to control the environment using a Dionysian approach.

- *Woodsmen:* An early counterforce to the Swordswoman (opposition of masculine and feminine), later they pair up with female figures to defend them (integration of masculine and feminine).

References

Bion, W.R. (1965) *Transformations.* London, UK: Heinemann Books.

Bion, W.R. (1963) *Elements of Psycho-Analysis.* London, UK: Heinemann Books.

Bion, W.R. (1962) *Learning from Experience.* London, UK: Heinemann Books.

Casement, Patrick (1991) *Learning from the Patient.* New York, NY: The Guilford Press.

Ferenczi, S. (1952) "The Origin of the Interest in Money." In *First Contributions to Psychoanalysis.* London, UK: Hogarth Press.

Fonagy, P; Gergely, G; Jurist, EL. and Target, M. (2002) *Affect Regulation, Mentalization, and the Development of the Self.* New York, NY: Other Press.

Kaufman, Y. (2009) *The Way of the Image: The Orientational Approach to the Psyche.* New York, NY: Zahav Books.

McPartland, J.C; Klin, A. and Volkmar F.R. (2014) *Asperger Syndrome: Assessing and Treating High-Functioning Autism Spectrum Disorders.* New York, NY: The Guilford Press.

Paglia, C. (1990) *Sexual Personae: Art and Decadence from Nefertiti to Emily Dickinson.* New York, NY: Vintage Books.

Trachtman, R. (1999) "The money taboo: Its effects in everyday life and in the practice of psychotherapy." *Clinical Social Work Journal 27,* 3, 275–288.

Young-Eisendrath, P., and Dawson, T. (1997). *The Cambridge Companion to Jung.* Cambridge, UK: Cambridge University Press.

CHAPTER FIVE

Subcutaneous, Subcortical, Subconscious and Subterranean

The Most Toxic Boy in the World's Search for Mum

Tim Woodhouse

Elliott looked up at his social worker and implored, "Why do you keep doing this to me? Why does nobody want me? It hurts, it hurts deep down, it hurts all the way down to the bottom." These were the words that choked seven-year old Elliott as his young social worker informed him that he would be moving him from his fifth foster placement. Macfie, Cicchetti, and Toth recognize that children in Elliott's situation struggle to make sense of their relationships as "maltreated children are more likely to have disorganized patterns of attachment to their caregivers in infancy, and deviant self-development, and develop an increasingly incoherent dissociated self during the pre-school period" (Macfie *et al.* 2001b, p.248). Howe noted "An adult or child with a history of unresolved loss and trauma has powerful emotions that remain unprocessed, unmetabolized and therefore untamed, destined to return again and again and not until such intense emotions can be linked to events, memories and conscious awareness can they be reflected upon, processed and contained" (Howe 2005, p.62). Without such integration, he argues that the child's identity is compromised, and importantly "cause-and-effect thinking, in which behaviour is understood to have consequences, is weak" (p.63). In other words, Elliott simply couldn't link his care receiving experiences, emotions, and bodily reactions or actions together. This sense of fragmentation and dissociation led to feelings of hopelessness and helplessness that any family was ever going to be able to contain him. The social worker felt a similar deep sense of helplessness and hopelessness that appeared to mirror the little boy's feelings.

Siegel (2010) cites Iacoboni (2008) in order to understand this phenomenon from a neuroscience perspective; that we use "cortical mirror neurons to detect and then simulate the internal state of another person" (p.37), the question remained however: whose feelings came first? The social worker had become aware that he was no longer the answer to the problem but part of the problem itself. Consumed with guilt and self-blame, and tortured by how Elliott had directed his hurt toward the social worker –"why do you keep doing this to me?" and the seemingly impossible to answer "why does nobody want me?"– it took a further two years to realize that what was being asked by Elliott could only have been answered by Elliott himself, and then only if he could have been enabled to go to where the pain stemmed from and hurt most: "deep down... all the way down to the bottom."

There was a knowledge gap for Elliott. He didn't know why he behaved, or a better word would be "acted," in the manner that he did, which ultimately led to his placement breakdowns. Truth is a misnomer for disassociative children with a skewed internal working model (Archer and Gordon 2006). They have a genuine "information gap" (p.105) and as such have difficulty in the recall of events. In addition Archer and Gordon note that "many traumatized children spend their days trying to avoid remembering distressing experiences and guarding against intrusive feelings" (p.62). For these children, survival means forgetting. There was also an information gap for the social worker who realized that a place of safety can only feel safe if the child can experience that safety from inside, deep down from the bottom.

"Alone. Yes, that's the key word, the most awful word in the English tongue. Murder doesn't hold a candle to it and hell is only a poor synonym" (King 1975, p.22).

Case Study: Oliver

Oliver was very much alone when I met him. He was five years old and was living in a temporary foster placement where he had resided since being removed from his parents two years previously due to the domestic violence, physical abuse, and grinding neglect he was exposed to during the course of his formative years. He was in a place of safety, living with a caring couple who had a long fostering career that bolstered their ability to provide for the children's complex needs. Oliver, however, wasn't safe. Every fibre of his body almost screamed at him, warning him that if he relaxed, relented, yielded, even just for a moment, he would be in danger and perhaps even die. Cozolino (2006) reflected on the deep nature of trauma in the statement; "the depth of harm caused by neglect, abuse, and inadequate nurturance rests on the fact that the human brain is a social organ. Relationships that cause pain teach children that their role in the group is tenuous, their existence is unnecessary, and their future survival is in question" (p.292) which arguably suggests that any cathartic process is going to have to, by definition, go equally deep in order to alleviate the distress or to bring about transformation.

Oliver's body and mind hadn't caught up with the notion that he was now safe, because he didn't feel safe, if indeed he ever had any concept of what safe meant. "When neither resistance nor escape is possible, the human system of self-defense becomes overwhelmed and disorganized. Every component of the ordinary response to danger, having lost its utility, tends to persist in an altered and exaggerated state long after the actual danger is over" (Herman 1992, p.34). He was perpetually triggered by frightening images and memories, that often stemmed from his five-sense perception linked to previous dangerous or frightening situations. These triggers were rarely obvious to the observer as they could be something almost imperceptible such as a particular colour, smell, sound or the prosody, volume, intonation or gender of a voice, a touch, temperature change or internal physical sensation, movement or movement failure. His baseline assessment concluded that his attachment pattern was disorganized (Main and Solomon 1990). He was quite simply living without a workable strategy to understand and survive relationships.

Because Oliver didn't feel safe he was extremely anxious. This anxiety probably led to a surge in stress hormones including adrenaline and cortisol. This tensed his muscles, over focused his vision as he became hyper-vigilant, dried his mouth, increased his heart rate and ventilation, raised his temperature, triggered profuse sweating, and produced an unpleasant odour from him. The anxiety was subcortical, almost within his skin. Within an instant these physiological symptoms took him out of his "window of tolerance" (Siegel 1999, p.253), or the capacity an individual has to self-regulate or at least be socially regulated. His "window" was not like that of a Georgian window: forgiving in its height and ample in width to cope with high stress, but pill-box narrow; defensive and limited, allowing the stress responses: freeze, flight, fight, feed, fart, and "attach-in-whatever-way-is-possible" to regularly take over with their myriad of behavioural or action symptoms that caused a familiar and therefore safer sense of chaos around him as his stress levels exceeded his small tolerance zone.

He wasn't afraid — he was terrified. But because it wasn't safe to show his fear he would become angry, aggressive and violent and, as Cairns (2002) points out, "anger, the emotion linked to rage and violence is a trance state. We are not clever or resourceful or kind or thoughtful when we are angry; we are just angry" (p.82) and in this instant Oliver wasn't thinking because thinking is a higher brain function that operates best when within the window of tolerance or the "optimum arousal zone" (Wilbarger and Wilbarger 1997 in Ogden, Minton and Pain 2006, p.27). At bedtime, when he was finally persuaded into bed, he couldn't settle and when he eventually did fall asleep he was tortured by night terrors, night sweats, and had frequent episodes of waking up in a semi-conscious and delirious state.

He hoarded food and ate without satiation, demonstrating a "nourishment barrier." There are people who commit to the lonely path of doing it all themselves. They don't expect any consistent support. They don't expect any real help from the outside. They don't expect nourishment. They have the view of the world as an empty place, where you can't count on anybody. When you offer nourishment, they reject it. They see something wrong with it. They won't take it in. As a result, they are never satisfied. They avoid taking in nourishment or even finding it in the world, because they do not want to deal with the possibility of loss. "The state of getting what you want is anxiety-producing. Having the thing so wanted leaves one vulnerable to losing it again. They're not good at taking in what's available" (Kurtz 1990, p.178).

Oliver did whatever he could do to feel safe; he bit, kicked out at adults and children alike, screamed, shouted, hurled abuse with colour, flurry, and venom. He hurled chairs, turned tables, ripped radiators from their housing, smashed flat screen TVs, skewered and tortured animals, urinated in every conceivable place in the house day and night, smeared feces targeting the foster carer's own children's bedrooms and possessions. Batmanghelidjh (2007) observed "every benign object in the service of your terror acquired dangers we had never anticipated" (p.40). This response was likely to be elicited equally by messages of love and nurture and care as it was by limits and boundaries and any response that contained a "no" message. Should the antecedent contain an implicit message of blame or shame, then the subsequent reaction was intensified. "The inner experience of shame is of painful exposure, transparency and vulnerability... when shame is disintegrative, it provokes instead the urge to hide, to build defensive strategies against the pain, and to attack the perceived source of the pain" (Cairns 2002, p.64).

When he couldn't fight, he ran, placing himself unconsciously and involuntarily into the dangers of high walls, roads, traffic, and people. He couldn't hear instruction because he couldn't pay attention. He was constantly bottom up hijacked by the lower, deeper, primeval, "bottom" parts of the brain and its familiar "get me out of gaol" quick response that bypassed any surface level cognition, narrative, processing, or analysis, and any chance of learning memory storage or memory retrieval. He was unwittingly and unknowingly using the depths of his brain to survive. Ogden et al. (2006, p.125) describe this type of "action system" as a "response to, or in anticipation of, an overwhelming or traumatizing event."

Oliver had experienced traumatic care-giving so frequently and regularly that his synapses had arguably hardwired to this response and thus he now responded to any negative or positive adult care-giving messages by defaulting to his parental experience. His caregivers and teachers set limits, boundaries and consequences, they praised when they could and told him repeatedly how to behave, but the messages, direction and limits fell without trace from his Teflon-coated ears. This left both caregivers and teachers alike confused, blaming, de-skilled and spent. They were filled with the same sense of helplessness and hopelessness that can spread like an airborne microbe debilitating all who came close to its source or into contact with those already infected.

Oliver couldn't trust because his map of the world reflected his care-receiving experience. In "good-enough" families newborn children receive hundreds and thousands of messages and actions that they are wanted or matter, are nurtured, loved and cared for that enable them to build a positive identity and thus meet others positively. Oliver's experience was devoid of these messages, and in addition he received messages of fear, pain, low warmth and high criticism, inconsistency and emotional and physical deprivation. His response to the judge for not allowing him to return home was to state "I'm going to kill him." His anger intensified; he scratched, bit, attempted to stab peers in school, swore, smashed property, and sexually assaulted other children. The map was written deep in his history, he was incubated in what was to come: the muffled sounds and sensations of violence, the raised maternal stress had increased her levels of stress hormones and those same high levels of maternal stress hormones that are associated with high levels of stress hormones in the fetus.

Wadhwa, Sandman and Garite (2001, p.138) provide preliminary evidence to support the notion that the influence of prenatal stress and maternal-placental hormones on the developing fetus may persist after birth, as assessed by measures of temperament and behavioural reactivity. The result for Oliver was a lower capacity for habituation and higher reactivity. He was gestated and born into a world of fear; any hope of assuagement, nurture, love, and acceptance dissipated as his mother's preoccupation with drugs took her emotionally further away than her pre-existing depression and violent relationship had already done.

Abandoned, he became responsible for his own survival and in order to survive he had to control his environment. For if you can't trust your mother how can you trust anyone else? His caregivers showed compassion and love and care toward Oliver as they had done to every child before him; however their love was not reciprocated but met instead with hate and spit and violence and destruction and anger that stemmed from his fear in an unrelenting tornado that had no amelioration or resolution, only exhaustion at the end for both the caregivers and Oliver. Their love, offered as freely as it was, hurt him more deeply than any abuse he had experienced as it only served to reinforce his belief that he wasn't loved by his own mother. He experienced his caregivers' love as a painful, perpetual reminder of not only his mother's abuse of him, but her lack of ability to love him, and thus his ultimate abandonment. Fear breeds fear from which no one could escape, with child, caregivers, teachers, and social workers alike sharing the same belief: the child was going to break the placement and that love would not grow here.

Oliver couldn't benefit from a talking therapy. His capacity to stay still was compromised as was his ability to pay attention and listen. In addition, he couldn't process the information because he couldn't create a narrative about a memory he didn't have. All he had was an implicit knowing that the world wasn't safe and the only way to manage that and keep safe was to run or fight: this is not about winning, but about survival. His screams were received as violence. Fear was camouflaged and hidden deep within and was missed. His tears were experienced by others as tears of anger and rage as opposed to sadness, fear, loss, and abandonment. Estes (1992) wrote: "A tear, heard by anyone of heart is a cry to come closer, tears not only represent feeling but are also lenses through which we gain an alternative vision, another point of view." It was almost as if those mirror neurons had failed to fire, and all that was seen or felt was his anger and not his pain.

Children need to be met by their therapist where they feel safest and the safest place is one that is known. Even if that place is the place where the child experienced the most pain, that pain at least is known to them, familiar and therefore safe. The unknown poses the greatest danger and thus the greatest threat, that with which children are unfamiliar allows their imagination to run untamed bringing up every possible fear that the child's imagination can conjure. The T.S. Elliot poems 'Four Quartets' suggest that the manner in which we start something is often the map as to how it will end and in some ways demonstrates the need to carefully prepare and lay the foundations that enable us to build a relationship that can weather the storms to come, but is also a relationship that will eventually come to an end. This action of meeting the child on their territory implicitly states; I am prepared to come to you, to see you and to hear you. The message we need to leave is that "I am prepared to wait for you to take that first step."

Sessions with Oliver

The first meeting revolved around a brochure lavish in pictures and frugal with words to give a basic rationale as to why we were meeting, what therapy is about and something about where it will take place. A decorated jam jar is also used with the child's name emblazoned on it, with a bag of marbles contained within. The purpose of the decorated jam jar is a simple acknowledgement that the child has been thought about and considered before the first meeting and that they have been held in mind. The marbles represent the number of sessions planned and thus the child can have some sense of time-scale and also this prepares them for endings. For longer intervention, the child is simply informed that we will talk about the need for further sessions every time the bag runs out of marbles. Oliver was pleased with the jar and commented that his name was on it. He then took me outside into the garden, climbed onto his trampoline, and bounced. As he bounced he stated "I can think when I bounce on here" to which he received the response "It's hard to think when you are standing still huh?" The amygdala is our built-in fire alarm (Ogden 2006 p.31) that detects danger and thus protects us from whatever that danger is, but it's not necessarily very good at distinguishing previous dangers, and things that remind us of those previous dangers, such as a snake and a stick or a harming parent from a safe parent. He didn't know that this up and down movement was impacting positively on his limbic system, helping to release endorphins into his system, but he knew it made a difference.

He stated, "You wouldn't want to come on here would you?" as he shook his head in anticipation of a re-buff. He faltered at the response "You're not sure if I'm the kind of grown-up that trampolines huh?" He opened the entrance in the netting and stepped back suddenly with a sense of doubt as he was joined on the unstable and wobbly platform and nodded at the observation "It's almost as though you are in two minds huh? Part of you wanted me to join in and the other wasn't so sure." We bounced.

The next time we met was at the clinic. He was brought by his caregiver, who waited in reception. Oliver grunted and made frequent facial expressions that distorted his face. His body misaligned with a significant curve with his chest pushed out as though at constant attention. He was rigid and held no sense of fluidity, almost as though he had little control over his own body. He was dyspraxic, unable to hear instruction and became increasingly hyper-kinetic with frenetic head shaking. He constantly manifested tension-reducing behaviours. He growled, yawned, and dissociated. He then came into the play therapy room.

The children's author A.A. Milne in his poem 'Disobedience' starkly describes the duty felt by a pseudo-parentified three-year-old who feels the responsibility to meet his mother's needs when his own are not met.

On entering the room Oliver imparted "I love my mummy, but she can't look after me." This statement suggested that he had made sense of attending therapy, and further suggested that in certain situations he was able to access his higher cortex and process information; however, this ability to think seemed to go off-line with ease and he was quickly triggered. In response to "And when you say you love your mummy, but she can't look after you, your body goes real tense, your head pulls back and you look as though you want to leave the room," his body tension reduced and his body movements calmed as his eyes went wide and he nodded. The follow up "It's almost as though you're wondering how you can love someone who can't look after you," led him to fill a castle with people and an attack with a huge dinosaur, demonstrating perhaps the chaos and danger of an unprotected environment. During this play, Oliver flatulated frequently (a stress response) which highlighted his anxiety and revealed how real this scenario felt to him.

There were many possible alternative responses that could have been made to Oliver's comment about his mother, but this was a gift. To ignore the importance might have fuelled his belief that these thoughts were off-limits; to reflect it back would have been safe but potentially trite. The danger of the given response could have been if it had been experienced as an interpretation and thus wrong. However, when we take the information we are given, accepting that this is their belief, we can take the child deeper and prevent getting stuck in a narrative. Play itself is often narrative. Scared children cannot be mindful, they are too busy trying to be safe and if they are not mindful then they cannot go deeper. To go deeper we need to have the capacity to self-regulate or have the capacity to be socially regulated (regulated by another). It was vital that the therapy not re-traumatize him and thus the early sessions were spent using every presented opportunity to resource him.

Resourcing activities that help the child stay in the "here and now," whilst observing the "there and then" do not need to be directive, stand-alone sessions out of context. In fact if the child has an information gap or finds it hard to process information, then this type of intervention is less likely to work, as the child is restricted in their ability to transfer one experience into a comparable situation in the future. Or in other words: the very reason they cannot "save to memory" in the first place is often the same reason they cannot retrieve information and utilize it in future situations or learn from their experience. If the child is helped to resource first, prior to their crisis, and later during their crisis where they feel and sense someone supporting their experience, this will be stored in the body, cortex, and feeling and context in a manner that has many access routes, rather than an implicitly cognitive route in which "taught" experiences have a habit of being stored. Resources that help, need to be practiced first in a situation where the child feels calm and can associate the experience with a calm state or the danger will be that when used solely in a crisis, the child may couple the resource to a negative-triggering event and reduce its efficacy.

Oliver made no representations of caregivers throughout the following weeks and months. His depictions of relationships were of other children he knew but had no connection with. The story stem exercise used as part of a baseline assessment graphically portrayed his lack of expectation of adult reciprocity, care-giving ability or desire that resulted in a lack of proximity and a dearth of love and nurture. This psychometric took him out of his "window of tolerance" (Siegel 1999, p.253) and appeared to prompt avoidant themes with the corollary of fatigue in both the child and mother doll, leading to avoidant behaviour, such as going to bed the moment breakfast was purported to be ready, but before it was consumed. There were attempts from the Oliver doll to call for the mother doll but she failed to hear and respond. In response to the lack of response, the child doll climbed on the roof, fell out of windows and/or was chased by spiders. His fear of adult proximity was matched by his generalized fear and distrust of all relationships. The mother doll was finally placed in sexually compromising situations with unscripted protagonists within the scenes. He stated that his mother "is not of this earth anyway." He had experienced blurred sexual boundaries and witnessed adult sexual behaviour. On occasion, when triggered at school, some of this sexual behaviour was acted out by Oliver toward his peers. This behaviour led to a real risk for both his peers and further risk to Oliver's safety as he became an easier target for exploitation. Because these incidents occurred when he was at his most stressed he had little recall of the events.

Houses and castles, forts and abodes were brought into his play in the weeks following the story, with representations of a tiny figure lost amidst the chaos, violence and danger. His anxiety was high which resulted in frequent toilet breaks. He was at the edge of his pain, a difficult place for both child and therapist to tolerate, as every instinct in human nature is to ameliorate, distract, pacify or avoid that pain. Ron Kurtz (1990, p.125) encouraged that we "ride the rapids," tolerating the ability to stay with a feeling that comes up in the moment. However, like the danger of narratives, we can get caught in a never-ending cycle of repetition and thus we need to funnel these feelings deeper to "mindfully experience deep emotion" (Ogden *et al.*, p.262).

Oliver was highly self-reliant but clearly in an insufficient way. He was working hard but simply couldn't go deeper, whilst he struggled living with caregivers who were not going to provide him with the permanence he craved and rejected in equal measure. Until he felt "claimed" he couldn't feel safe enough to go to the depths.

Therapy often needed to be deeper than subcortical as anything spoken was likely to be missed, misunderstood, experienced as unclear, or misinterpreted as a threat or a slight. Oliver was eventually transferred into another foster placement and in therapy his play quickly developed. He started to dig in the wet sand tray and created an island upon which he placed a child figure and stated, "I'm on my own." His response to "Sometimes we can be in a class, a crowded room or a new family and still feel alone huh?" was to bury other figures. He found a sarcophagus containing an embalmed mummy that came to be an enduring metaphor for his search for a safe mother, as well as a fear of his birth mother and other women in a care-giving role in general. He began to bury the sarcophagus but, no matter how often he buried it, the mummy would escape and chase the boy. Alone, the boy ran and not even a squad of police officers could prevent the mummy from chasing him, and worse the officers repeatedly fell to their peril from ravines, cliff edges, ropes or ledges into shark infested oceans, bogs, sinking sand with its lurking "sand-man," toxic waste and human effluence, demonstrating how the police could not even take care of themselves let alone the little boy.

He needed to go deeper than the sand tray allowed and so transferred his play to a deep sandbox. He dug and dug and as he dug his concentration focused and his dyspraxia subsided. The energy required to dig seemed to have a calming effect on his body and mind. The sarcophagus was buried at the bottom and two police officers were again sent to stand guard. Still the mummy emerged, overcame the officers and sought the boy who hid. In many respects this was a true depiction of his life. Terrified by his mother, he was eventually taken to a place of safety by the police. However the police were then unable to prevent him being taken back every week to have contact with the person who frightened him most. Although contact had long-since been stopped, his fear of being returned to his mother was equal to his fear of not being claimed by a mother capable of containing him, wanting him, or loving him. Oliver believed now that his placements were incapable of these things and was more afraid of not knowing when they would end than the end of the placement itself...so he strove to end the placement. However, as in the words of the 1965 Bob Dylan song "Subterranean Homesick Blues," it was the repetitive nature of his behaviour that caused it, something he seemed responsible for, but that wasn't in Oliver's case a conscious choice. When the placement ultimately disrupted, it was as though he had succeeded, even though in reality he had no understanding of his presenting behaviour.

And he arguably succeeded. Oliver was eventually moved to another foster placement and when he next came to therapy he made no mention of the move. He buried the mummy in the deepest place before turning his attention toward me. He went to the dressing up box where he found an abundance of weapons and proceeded for the next few months to shoot, stab, slice, disembowel, disembody, poison, explode, set on fire, and bury his therapist. When his actions and pain were reflected back to him he took a Zippy puppet (Zippy was a fictional character on the British children's television program *Rainbow*. Zippy was a brownish-orange puppet with a rugby-ball-shaped oval head, blue eyes, and a zip for a mouth that was often zipped closed.) Oliver zipped its mouth shut while staring into my eyes and stuffed Zippy into a pot, screwed the lid on and taped it shut. The response "Showing me how much it hurts when someone has a voice and you don't; you would like me not to have a voice either" led to a cold stare and further annihilation in a myriad of ways. His creativity and repertoire in the murder of the other was impressive in its diversity and extent.

The mantra of no therapy until a child is safe is ultimately correct. Being in transition is akin to not being safe. Both are strong edicts that should always be considered and prioritized. That said, under that particular premise there are a number of children who, due to their circumstances, would not get treatment until they have passed the point of no return, becoming adolescents who have learnt not to engage. If, however, the child has been in placement a while and there is time to build a relationship before a planned move, then therapeutic intervention is possible. Oliver demonstrated that he was still able to explore the deepest reaches of his psyche, despite the challenges he presented to those who tried to come close, in every other aspect of his life. He stopped killing his therapist.

The mummy re-emerged after her long burial: *La mère est morte, vive la mère.* The mother, charged with the care of two children continued to frighten and neglect them until they were once again taken away by the police, returned to her care, removed, returned, removed, returned... and he dug. The maximum depth humans have achieved underground is at the Western Deep Levels gold mine in the Transvaal, South Africa, but deeper in the ocean (Piccard and Dietz 1961), and Oliver seemed determined to go deeper than either. The next time he dug, he buried the child figure, enlisting my help to shore up the sides of his deep mausoleum and ensure the child doll was incarcerated. He stated "He's the most poisonous boy in the world." Briere's "abuse dichotomy" (1992, p.27) eloquently describes how when faced by abuse from the very person charged with the responsibility of keeping a child safe, in order to prevent seeing the child's own parent/carer as bad then the child must see themselves as the cause. For everyone, our understanding of whom we are and our place in the world, how we relate to those around us, as well as those in the wider world is critical to our emotional well-being. Levy and Orlans(1998) note, "Identity is who the child believes him or herself to be. Identity formation is based on the child's experiences, or interpretation of those experiences, other's reactions to the child, and the significant role models the child identifies with" (p.368).

The desire to escape the pain of the child, to rescue him, even though the message was projected safely onto the child figurine is often agonizingly intense, but this was a belief and beliefs are learnt early in our development even when we are only a stone's throw away in years as Oliver was at that time. "It seems like he believes that huh?" was the reflection and following a nod of agreement, "I wonder when he first learnt that he was the most poisonous boy in the world?" to which he responded "I'm bad, I'm bad to the bones" whilst lifting his t-shirt and showing his prominent ribcage, as though I would be able to see the badness he felt. His greatest fear at the bottom of the abyss, where his dangerous persona lies buried, deep within the lower primeval brain where survival lurks and thinking abates, he hit the bottom. When we reach the foundation, the underbelly, we are faced with our core beliefs and in that moment he let go of the need of a metaphor or a projective figurine and shared his belief; his fear. He cried.

There is a moment in Golding's Lord of the Flies (1954 p.89) when the character Simon starts to question the origin of the beast as an external entity and begins to inwardly reflect. Like all disorganized children, there is no inner beast and no being born bad or evil, yet this is a message that their behaviour can promote or persuade others to believe, and it is certainly a belief that the child learns to own…to fit. Self-loathing arose out of the depths of his pain, for if it cannot be the fault of the father, the mother, or the other, then who else is left but the self? At home and in therapy he continued to dig. His dens at home reflected a need to find safety but also to bury part of himself: his poison, his toxicity, his shit. He buried his feces. Sometimes he would share his poo dens with unwary visitors and sometimes he kept them to himself, perhaps as a reminder of his own existence, or his own dangerousness and toxicity. In therapy he finally relinquished his need to be self-reliant and abandoned his attempts to push away or kill his therapist off and instead enlisted the therapist's help to create the deepest holes. So why when the belief has been uncovered does the dig continue? When children are stuck they need repetition to make sense of their beliefs and to confront the meaning behind that belief which can be debilitating. For Oliver it would mean facing his parents' inability to meet his needs.

"Dig" implored Oliver, "dig or we will die." "It seems as though our lives depend on it huh? When you have that thought that we must dig or we will die, what do you notice happening in your body?" Oliver noticed nothing, despite his body held rigid, the flatulence choking the life out of the room and a pungent smell emitting from his skin. "It's almost as though you don't notice how hot you get when you think about dying huh?" He stopped and turned toward me and said, "Tim, we need to talk" and ushered his therapist to the couch. In a moment it seemed he had moved from being a tiny child to an old man. He said, "You don't think I should live with my mum, do you?" When a child asks a question it usually means that they are ready to hear the answer. Sometimes we cannot give the child the whole story at this point, as it may be potentially damaging, but the response must be based on the truth. He had made it back up to the surface, in his higher cortex, his attention, his hearing, his thinking, processing, analytic mind was back online, at least for the moment. "No, I don't think you should see your mother. I think she has great difficulty looking after herself let alone a little boy" to which his swift riposte was "But I'm bigger now, I can look after her and me," as he slipped back into his pseudo-parentified, self-reliant strategy.

"I know you will be angry with me, but I would rather you be angry with me and safe than not angry and unsafe." He sat in silence. "I want to see if that very young boy, that little Oliver can hear some words that I'm going to say to him, and I want you to notice what happens when you hear those words, is that ok?" He nodded his approval. "I don't know why your mummy and daddy did the things that they did because I wasn't there, but I do know that every little boy deserves to be looked after in the best way possible and not to have to feel afraid or believe that they are poisonous or bad." His head dropped for a moment, then looked up and stated "I get hot when I think about my mum and I get hotter when I see her." "Wow, you noticed how hot you get when you think about your mum or see her, and when you notice that heat in your body does an image or a memory come up?" Again he thought for a moment and said, "I remember blood, lots and lots of blood... was there blood?" "It seems as though you remember blood huh? And when you remember that blood what do you notice?" "There was a lot of blood. There was blood everywhere" he retorted and asked, "Was it me?"

Now we don't ever know the whole truth, but psycho-education is part of our responsibility to help understanding when a child is showing signs of being able to process and wants clarification on the truth, no matter how hard that truth can sometimes be. The fear that a child imagines is often worse than the reality, but clearly great care must be taken when that information is shared and how much is appropriate to share at any given time. "I don't know what happened in your family because I wasn't there, but I do know that your mum hurt herself a lot." "Did she do it with a knife?" he quickly asked. "Yes," I replied, "she did it with a knife." Then he stated "I know she did... there was so much blood." And then he sobbed, the deep pain of fear, and loss, and relief.

Oliver came into the reception of the clinic for the next session and hid. The search for Oliver began and the caregiver was enlisted to help look for him. The hunt was a balance in that he must not be found too quickly as the healthy giggle and excitement of anticipation of being found needed to be experienced, enjoyed, and "hung-out with," but so too should the finding not be too late for fear the child gives up hope and feeds into the sense of lurking abandonment. As his excitement grew his developmental age regressed and on his being found, his response to the caregiver was warm, affectionate, and yielding. He entered therapy satisfied.

He went straight to his snack, the same snack he had been provided throughout the period of therapy that he had eaten thus far without comment. He took the wrapper off, bit into the biscuit and stopped. "Noticed something, huh?" His eyes wide, staring straight toward and meeting my eyes, he nodded before declaring, "That's lovely. That's the nicest biscuit I have ever tasted." As his stress levels reduced his ability to access five-sense perception increased and his ability to taste, for so long compromised, appeared to come back online.

Oliver abandoned the physical act of digging after this and instead tentatively began to involve his therapist in role-play. This took his play into metaphorical digging and hiding and into the exploration of tunnels to new and scary worlds. The fear now had changed in its quality and moved from undead mummies, snakes, and monsters to expectations, such as: what did the world want from him and could he meet or survive those expectations. He entered into increasingly collaborative work and whilst the subterranean theme endured for a long while, it was as though he was making his way back to the surface. He continued to struggle with relationships and stress would pre-empt the triggering of his old strategies, but his regressions would become less pronounced and shorter in duration as he began to slowly re-surface and face the reality of the pain that relationships stirred up in him.

At school he stopped targeting weaker vulnerable children as well as trying to engage in sexual activity with his peers. As he began to feel safer he became less prone to attack but at this point the abuse dichotomy emerged. As Oliver emerged from his trauma-induced lower brain state and started to use his higher cortex with increasing ease, he became aware of just how far academically he lagged behind his peers. He was exposed to his sense of shame, which he managed to the degree that it didn't debilitate him but none-the-less highlighted his sense of vulnerability. His peers, however, sensed the tide change and moved from victims to victimizers in an almost oceanic swell. Despite the onslaught, he didn't return to his default fight, flight, or sexual responses but lamented how no one – not caregivers, social workers, teachers, or therapists could help him as he dove into hypo-arousal and sadness.

Like many children in this position of such dramatic change he believed his only chance was to leave the school. He believed a fresh start would allow him to re-invent himself. This is not dissimilar to how ordinarily developing children leaving primary or preparatory education often reinvent themselves going into high school, or from high to college, and so on. Change is rarely positive for children with a history of disruption and transition and a disorganized attachment – except for when it is.

Over the later sessions his body began to noticeably relax, the tension that had deformed his body reduced and his tics and involuntary movements subsided. During one role-play vignette he devised that required a particularly tight and long journey through a shapeless Lycra tunnel into a strange new world, he gently touched my arm to bring my attention to his gaze as he whispered with glee, "There is treasure to be had and there is enough for both of us!"

His fingers and hands for the first time were cool to the touch and the smell that emitted from his pores evaporated. His ability to seek proximity and hold the gaze of another were indicators that his anxiety had reduced, bringing down his body temperature, slowing down his physical responses, broadening his vista, and enabling him to develop a shared narrative. As he took the treasure he celebrated, stating, "Now everyone can be happy as there is enough love for everyone." There were no more murders, deaths, mutilations, sacrificial burnings, or decapitations at the end of his sessions. Instead, he began to experiment ending the sessions with making it back to the world of reality just in time for our goodbyes and the collapse of the imaginary world behind him. He met his caregiver at the end of the sessions with a spontaneous hug, where he melted into her arms and breast and yielded to her safety – he had found a safe mum.

"Is it time to take my marble jar home?" asked Oliver. "It seems like you know it's nearly time to say to say goodbye? And when you notice that it's nearly time to say goodbye Oliver, is there a feeling that comes up?" "Yes," said Oliver "I feel sad that I won't see you again, but happy that I don't need to come anymore." "Let's hang out with that happiness for a while before we say goodbye for ever," I suggested… he nodded… And we did.

References

Archer, C. and Gordon, C. (2006). *New Families, Old Scripts: A Guide to the language of trauma and attachment in adoptive families.* London, UK: Jessica Kingsley Publishers

Batmanghelidjh, C. (2007) *Shattered Lives: Children Who Live with Courage and Dignity.* London, UK: Jessica Kingsley Publishers.

Cairns, K. (2002). *Attachment, Trauma and Resilience: Therapeutic Caring for Children.* London, UK: BAAF.

Briere, J. (2011) *TSI–2: Trauma Symptom Inventory–2: Professional manual.* Florida: PAR.

Cozolino,L.(2006) *The Neuroscience of Human Relationships: Attachment and the Developing Social Brain.* New York, NY: W.W. Norton.

Dylan, B. (1965) *Subterranean Homesick Blues.* [CD]. New York, NY: Columbia Records.

Eliot, T. S. (1943) *Four Quartets.* New York, NY: Harcourt.

Estes, C.P. (1992) *Women Who Run with the Wolves: Contacting the Power of the Wild Woman.* London, UK: Rider.

Golding, W. (1954) *Lord of the Flies.* London, UK: Faber and Faber.

Herman, J.L. (1992). *Trauma and Recovery.* New York, NY: Basic Books.

Howe, D.(2005) *Child Abuse and Neglect: Attachment, Development and Intervention.* Basingstoke, UK: Macmillan.

Iacoboni, M. (2008) *Mirroring People.* New York, NY: Farrar, Straus and Giroux.

King, S. (1975) *Salem's Lot.*

King, S. (1978) *The Stand.* New York, NY: Doubleday.

Kurtz,R.(1990) *Body-Centered Psychotherapy: The Hakomi Method.* Mendocino, CA: LifeRhythm Press.

Levy, T. M. and Orlans, M. (1998) *Attachment Trauma and Healing: Understanding and Treating Attachment Disorder in Children and Families.* Washington, DC: AEI Press.

Macfie, J., Cicchetti, D. and Toth, S. (2001a) The development of dissociation in maltreated preschool-aged children. *Development and Psychopathology, 13,* 233–254.

Macfie, J.; Cicchetti, D. and Toth, S. (2001b) "Dissociation in maltreated versus nonmaltreated preschooler-aged children." *Child Abuse and Neglect, 25,* 1253–1267.

Main, M. and Solomon, J. (1986) "Discovery of an Insecure-Disorganized/Disoriented Attachment Pattern: Procedures, Findings and Implications for the Classification of Behavior." In T. B. Brazelton and M. Yogman (eds) *Affective Development in Infancy.* Norwood, NJ: Ablex.

Main, M. and Solomon, J. (1990) In M. T. Greenberg, D. Cicchetti and M. Cummings (eds) *Procedures for identifying infants as disorganized/disoriented during the Ainsworth Strange Situation. Attachment in the Preschool Years: Theory, Research, and Intervention* (pp. 121–160). Chicago, IL: The University of Chicago Press.

Milne, A.A. (1926) *Winnie-The-Pooh.* London, UK: Methuen and Co.

Milne, A.A. (1924) "The Wrong House" in *When We Were Very Young.* London, UK: Methuen.

Milne, A.A. (1924) "Disobedience" *When We Were Very Young.* London, UK: Methuen.

Ogden, P; Minton, K. and Pain, C. (2006) *Trauma and the Body: A Sensorimotor Approach to Psychotherapy.* London, UK: W.W. Norton.

Piccard, Jacques and Dietz, Robert S. (1961) *Seven Miles Down: The Story of the Bathyscaph.* Trieste, Italy: G.T. Putnam's Sons.

Siegel, D. (1999) *The Developing Mind: Toward a Neurobiology of Interpersonal Experience.* New York, NY: Guilford Press.

Siegel, D. J. (2010) *The Mindful Therapist: A Clinician's Guide to Mindsight and Neural Integration.* New York, NY: W.W. Norton.

Wadhwa P.D, Sandman C.A, and Garite T.J. (2001) "The neurobiology of stress in human pregnancy: Implications for prematurity and development of the fetal central nervous system". *Pubmed 133,* 131–142.

CHAPTER SIX

Out of the Box and Into the Wild

Therese Bimka

*Dedicated to my son Dylan Bimka Wintrob who
helps me keep my heart open and alive.*

Deep play implies deep contact – a soul-full invitation for the essential Self to come out and play. Author and philosopher Parker Palmer (2004) says the soul is like a wild animal – shy and reluctant to emerge without certain parameters. Accessing the depths, as the title of this book implies, calls for a profound sense of safety, freedom, and a willingness to listen from the heart. When this field is activated, the soul and spirit are willing to peek out and engage.

As a clinician, I never fit neatly into a box. Earlier in my career, this used to be a source of discomfort as I sought to find "my tribe" within my own profession. But as is often the case, my professional identity was mirroring a fundamental truth of my life: I have always found inspiration through a diversity of sources, often "outside the box" of mainstream culture. Over the years this discomfort became quieter, less primary. I was deeply nourished by the work itself, particularly by the clients I seemed to attract – many of whom were also hungry for tools that were "out of the box," innovative and integrative. To nurture myself and to serve my clients, I pursued a wide range of training – with some modalities spanning more than a decade – as I searched for models of healing and transformation that felt big enough to hold a larger, more complex story of the human condition and to hold my own story.

Since my twenties, I have had a number of professional identities: professional ceramic artist, art teacher, psychotherapist, interfaith minister, and most recently spiritual counselor and director. All of these professional explorations have confirmed and reconfirmed my core belief that manifested when I was younger and continues to this day: that the breadth and depth of the human condition is steeped in complexity – a textured quilt of familial and cultural conditioning, innate temperament, exposure to life's curriculum, and archetypal energies seeking to emerge. All this and so much more interfaces with the great mystery of human transformation and divine possibility. One portal, one lens or system of understanding cannot capture this magnificent quilt. It is this beauty that I seek to embrace in my work with children and adults. I look for vehicles of engagement that can honor this stunning complexity and not inadvertently diminish it in the pursuit of healing and transformation. This continues to be a source of deep inquiry for my work as a psychotherapist and as a spiritual counselor and director.

To this end, I have taken my inspiration from several modalities, or what one might call portals of clinical and spiritual engagement, the most prominent ones being: Jungian sandplay therapy, Soulcollage®, expressive arts, and a variety of mindfulness based practices. These work on the body-mind-spirit level using guided visualizations and meditation. And for several years, since I became an ordained minister, I have been fascinated by the interface between psychological healing and spiritual longing and development.

In my experience, I have found that change is only possible in the present moment, which is why the experiential modalities, some of which cited above, are so effective. These present-centered modalities can access and identify what is alive or needing care and attention in the here and now. The underlying premise of this orientation is a fundamental trust that the psyche will self-regulate the work. In other words – whatever shows up for healing is exactly what needs attention and/or recalibration to make room for the next leg of the journey. It is a non-pathological approach steeped in the vital belief of the psyche's drive towards self-actualization and wholeness that Jung identified as innate to the human condition (Jung *et al.* 1973, 1964).

Over the years, the following core concepts have crystallized as essential to my work and my understanding of transformation:

- Seeing clients as whole and intact despite areas of limitation

- Trusting the innate drive towards wholeness which includes a belief in the fundamental resilience of the psyche and the innate wisdom within that is always available

- Having an understanding of psyche that allows for the multiplicity of self (the many aspects of self based on our personal life stories and the more universal archetypal stories)

- A core belief in the healing power of a loving, authentic, attuned relationship for attachment "repair," honoring our innate longing to belong

- Valuing the necessity of unstructured play and the cultivation of curiosity

- The necessity for silence and slowing down in an increasingly noisy and accelerated world

- The healing power of nature and the elements

- The idea that various portals of engagement are open and receptive for transformation at different times along the way offering avenues for focus and meaningful engagement

- The importance of the union of opposites for healing and nourishing the individuation journey

- The importance of integrating the shadow

- The belief that all symptoms are teleological, i.e purposeful

- The belief that our unique gifts are exactly what the world needs (inspired by the work of Malidoma Some (1994))

- The transformative value of the imagination

- The perspective that virtually all psychiatric imbalances can be understood in terms of too much chaos or too much rigidity (I was delighted to read that Dr. Daniel Siegel (2007) offers this perspective in his book on the Mindful Brain as this has been my intuitive point of view as a clinician for many years).

The limitations of language and the symbolic value of myths and archetypes

As clinicians, while we attempt to use language in the mysterious process of healing, the work of transformation can sometimes feel intangible, hard to name and challenging to capture. It helps to have a rudder to the ship. Myths and archetypes offer such a rudder and seem to spontaneously arise when their service is needed.

Seena Frost, founder of SoulCollage® offers a myth that is relevant for our time – that of Indra's Net. This myth from the Avatamaka Sutra of the Mahayana Buddhist tradition of Second Century India, seems to hold valuable teachings for this particular historical juncture where Frost, and others, say the wisdom of the feminine is on the rise. In her book Evolving SoulCollage® (2010), Frost describes The Net of Indra as a metaphor for the complexity and totality of creation: from the macro to the micro. In the ancient texts, Indra's net is described as infinite, spreading over and connecting all of creation. Adorning the net are jewels. "Each jewel reflects all others infinitely" (Frost, p.177) that also serve to reflect the innate wisdom within.

There are a number of symbolic teachings in the bejeweled net but for the purposes of this chapter the one that may be most relevant is the holographic nature of the jewels. As in all symbols, the part reflects and captures the whole and is a whole in and of itself. This is a key concept in symbolic processes like Jungian sandplay therapy and Soulcollage®. The net also describes one of the guiding principles of Soulcollage® – The One and The Many. The One refers to universal source or essence and The Many refers to the diverse range of archetypal expressions within the multiplicity of self. The One and The Many represent in essence the human condition.

I have found Soulcollage® a complimentary modality to Jungian sandplay. Both modalities use imagery and symbolism to capture the receptive energy within the psyche, primed and ready for emergence and evolution. While sandplay uses miniatures, sand, and the container of the sandbox, Soulcollage® uses 2-dimensional imagery, 5x7 inch (12.5 x 17.5 cm) cards for collaging and then journal writing to dialogue with the images. In my work with children, I have used the MeCards approach developed by Weiss and Raphael (2013) which is a modification of the method for children.

Frost has encouraged the Soulcollage® community to create and adorn their own Indra Net as a living symbol for the beauty of our work. It is a useful metaphor, as a net can both capture what is essential or core for living and it can be a symbol of our interconnectedness as in the web of life. It affirms the multiplicity of self – from the personal story to the various archetypes living in us and seeking expression through us.

Jung, who first identified that deep within all of us are multiple aspects of self (archetypes) that carry both life affirming energies and shadow. Both poles hold important gifts and energy needed for vitality and embodied living. Integrating these polarities (union of opposites) is what fuels and supports the individuation process – Jung's term for the innate drive towards wholeness. This belief that we are fundamentally whole, alongside or within our imperfections, is the single most important belief that fuels my work. From this vantage point, everything is possible and all "symptoms" are useful or purposeful and in the service of transformation. They represent a universal dance that supports our psychological and spiritual evolution.

When a clinician is able to access and witness the core Self of the client – transformation unfolds with greater ease and speed. It happens even faster when the clinician is in touch with his or her own core Self and sense of wholeness. This creates a resonant field of possibility.

Jung stated that the Self archetype is "the archetype of wholeness and the regulating center of the psyche." (Sharp 1990, p.190). For Jung, the Self archetype (often described as the divine Self, the wisdom Self, the core or essential Self) contains the energy needed for meaningful engagement and purposeful drive. It is the working synthesis of the Self archetype and the ego that facilitates the individuation process. Jung identified the innate drive towards our own wholeness as existing *a priori* – an innate drive that is universal. It is a universal pattern that is part of our human blueprint. According to Jung, it is through the individuation process that we move closer and closer to our true Self, to our most authentic inner core.

Accessing the Self archetype is essential to all healing but when this is done *in relationship*, the possibility of transformation is heightened. Psychotherapist and Buddhist teacher Tara Brach (2003) talks eloquently about the fundamental need to be seen and known in our essential Self as one of the most important universal human needs. It is also the place of wounding and disconnection, especially when who we truly are is not seen, valued, or accepted. In our essence, we are inter-dependent beings. We need others to reflect us accurately (especially as children) so we can learn to rest in our authenticity and let it guide our growth and development.

In working with children, I have come to appreciate that within even the most intact and loving home environments the ego self gets wounded by the simple act of interfacing with the world. This causes the core Self to go into hiding. It seems inevitable.

Psychotherapist, Buddhist teacher, and author John Welwood talks about this phenomenon in his book *Love and Awakening*:

> We all enter the world possessing an intrinsic radiance that shines forth from our inner core. We are born into a vast palace of powers and possibilities; our being contains boundless potential...[but] when the adult world – either through misunderstanding, neglect, or outright abuse – fails to see or value us as children, we feel deeply hurt. Our soul experiences a kind of shock, which closes down [or dampens] the natural openness and [aliveness] of our being... The child is like an open hand that gradually starts to contract and close. (Welwood 1996, pp.10 and 12).

The closed hand metaphor is a good one as it captures the natural response in psyche to pain or conflict which is to contract or flinch. When we begin to live in the contraction as a primary way to manage and deal with pain and discomfort it becomes problematic. This is often when children become symptomatic and come into treatment.

This constriction can take many forms from physiological patterns held in the body to "ways of being" that are rigid (for example – rigid ideas, opinions, belief systems or feeling states). Any form of constriction creates a stoppage of energy, chi, or flow. This stoppage begins to accumulate debris whether psychic or physiological, which in turn further restricts access to our aliveness or potential. In my experience, the more rigid the symptom, the more vulnerable the client. I often use metaphors or guided visualizations that activate flexibility to counter-balance the encroaching rigidity. Even children seem to understand instinctively that inner flexibility fosters resiliency and makes healing and transformation possible.

Two clinical case study overviews
Case Study: Julia

For a number of years, I have been working with young girls who have big imaginations. What I have observed is that these extraordinary imaginations offer a profound source of joy and self-connection that is rich and inspired. But the shadow side of this gift is that living in and finding joy in the world can be challenging for these young souls. The "real world" is often experienced as a disappointment, where the requirement to conform can feel toxic to the free-flowing imaginal energy of the psyche. In essence, the energetic power of these big and active imaginations is often in conflict with the need to function in this world.

Being in the world can be hard work for these girls and yet it is my belief that the world desperately needs the gifts that these young girls represent and embody – a sort of wild woman/girl archetypal energy that refuses to conform, to fit in a box or to limit the creative possibilities of their soul and spirit. Helping these young girls find their way in the world without losing their essential gifts or having their vibrant imaginations "schooled out of them" is a task I willingly embrace with great care and humility.

When Julia (pseudonym) first came to see me I was captivated by her creative energy that flowed freely, seemingly without restraint. Over the years of working together, Julia has used a number of creative modalities to express her inner reality (paint, ritual, poetry and Soulcollage®), but it was Jungian sandplay therapy that was the most effective tool for her unfolding. In the sand, her stories found their voice. Week after week mythic tales expanded and contracted, mirroring the cosmic dance of the universe. There seemed to be a deep recognition that in sandplay Julia could finally play in a manner that was fully engaged, no holds barred. Like a fish to water, she immersed herself in the unfolding story of her own healing process with abandon. Here she was free to spread her wings and soar or descend, listening for and responding to whatever her psyche and spirit longed for. As she dove into the sanctuary of the sandplay room, it was clear that her spirit finally felt at home. One could almost hear a deep sigh of relief.

For the purposes of this chapter, I will extrapolate two metaphors that emerged in her work as they are key to the theme of deep play and transformation: the descent into the underworld and the subsequent creation of hibernation chambers.

Julia came to therapy as an eight-year-old with a vibrant inner life but she was stifled in the external world of relationships. We forged a safe and loving bond where her smart, funny, and poignant stories could unfold with all the drama and excitement of a full Broadway production. But this was not leisure or recreational time – this was soul time and her psyche was busy at work. One can always tell when the psyche is really working as there is a purposefulness to the play that is palpable.

As time passed and when enough therapeutic safety had been established, Julia began an important piece of work. She was ready for a descent. This is an important development in the sandplay journey, for it is in the depths that one can access the core Self. Julia announced that she needed to prepare for her descent into the underworld (her language). Her previous trays had been focused on various myths – mostly Greek and Roman gods and goddesses. Her work in the sand thus far had prepared her to go deeper. So when the underworld beckoned, Julia said yes. The vehicle of her descent was the biggest snake in my miniature collection.

The snake is a complicated symbol, embodying great polarities and controversy. In western culture, it is frequently misunderstood as a villain separating original man and woman from their divine connection with God in the Garden of Eden, through the promise of forbidden knowledge. For Native Americans the snake is viewed as an ancient symbol of healing and transformation. In Eastern traditions, the snake can represent the coiled "life force" asleep at the base of the spine seeking to be released. Known as Kundalini energy, the sleeping serpent can activate big energy in the service of awakening innate creativity and vitality.

As a member of the reptile family, the snake represents one of the oldest life forms on the planet. Reptiles have survived for millions of years and are considered highly adaptable (Andrews 1993). As cold-blooded creatures, they rely on the external environment to survive, seeking environments that can help regulate their body heat. Symbolically, this implies a great sensitivity to external stimuli and can result in being overly adaptable to external circumstances or extremely selective (read "rigid"), which seemed to make sense where Julia was concerned.

Additionally, the shedding of one's skin and the regeneration that follows were also significant for Julia at this stage in her development. The shedding of the old can also refer to letting go of what no longer serves. As we grow and expand, old systems and ways of being may literally be too small for the new self seeking to emerge. In the shedding process, the old self makes room and allows the new self to breathe itself into existence. In this regard, the snake is an ally and a symbol for the metamorphosis and evolution of the core Self.

As an eight-year-old, Julia was preoccupied with the question: "What does one pack for a journey to the underworld?" and indeed, packing and preparing for the descent was the focus of a half a dozen trays (Figure 6.1). There were trunks filled to the brim with tools, books and miscellaneous items. Many vessels were overflowing with food and other forms of sustenance. There was furniture, as she did not know how long she would be staying "down there." It seemed the snake was setting up residence. I always find children to be incredibly resourceful and ultimately very practical.

Figure 6.1: Packing for the Underworld

Following the underground descent, the work morphed into the creation of delightful hibernation chambers that were both whimsical and elaborate, each one created with precise attention to detail. In fact, it often took a whole session to create just one chamber (Figure 6.2). What was equally touching was how cozy these chambers were, especially important as they always housed an array of little babies (Figure 6.3).

Figure 6.2: Hibernation Chambers   *Figure 6.3: The Babies Emerge*

It is interesting that there is a connection between snake symbolism and the hibernation baby chambers. First, the descent to the underworld is often understood as a death/birth/rebirth cycle. Death can refer to the end of old ways of being. Additionally, the goddess Vinita is associated with the death/birth and the underworld (Eason 2007, p.21) and in Hindu cosmology, there are a number of serpent goddesses who are associated with birth. I love when literature supports and enhances what is organically emerging in the children's play.

Julia's babies represented all ages and stages of development. Some seemed newborn, as if emerging for the very first time, and older ones seemed to symbolize already present, yet still with vulnerable aspects of the self that needed to incubate. Knowing when and how to protect these vulnerable aspects is a cornerstone of resiliency vital to growth and development. Julia was using her time in the sand well.

Week after week, I witnessed the babies lovingly placed in these chambers of protected and functional stasis. They seemed to be waiting for a signal indicating when it would be safe to emerge. Perhaps Julia first had to grow a more resilient "skin" so she was less porous and susceptible to the challenging energies of the world around her, which she often experienced as disturbing. In a quiet and symbolic way, Julia seemed to know innately that when one is ready to shed old ways of being that are no longer working, it can be a very vulnerable time. It is a "between" time — representing a time before a new skin develops or new strategies are realized. This seemed to be the task at hand and the chambers were the perfect solution. Julia continued her work demonstrating the wonderful resiliency and resourcefulness of her imagination.

After several months of chamber building — she indicated that perhaps she no longer needed the hibernation chambers. At this time, her stories began to focus on young girls who had mastered their magical powers and had learned to use their power selectively. It seemed the babies were growing up. Part of their empowerment involved knowing when to hide their gifts, which I think is a real life lesson and an excellent piece of discernment for Julia, and for girls in general. It can be dangerous for girls to show their strength and power in the world and this discernment seemed to be a lesson Julia learned from both the descent and the hibernation chambers.

As her girls became more visible and powerful, she too became more courageous and assertive — growing in self-assurance. The humor of the descent (what shall I pack?) became a wonderful trademark for much of her subsequent work and play. She learned to use her humor and sharp wit to create meaning and connection with the world. Humor and wit became woven into her new resilient skin supporting a more flexible and responsive stance in the world. The sand and its symbols held and nourished the deep journey down, towards the core Self that helped Julia birth and forge a unique identity as someone with great imaginative capacity and wit. This dynamic duo will serve her well in this world.

In closing, I would like to share a poignant metaphor that emerged during one of her sand stories. About one year after her hibernation chambers, while she was still working with her magical "empowerment" girls: "If you don't love your wings, they won't flourish and grow. They'll remain small and not that useful." So true. Yet, in order to "love our wings" we all need a place where we can spread them out in all their splendor. Paradoxically, accessing the depths to mine the treasures from below directly correlates to our capacity to soar. In fact, the height of our flight can be measured by the depth of our descent. Through deep archetypal metaphor, Jungian sandplay therapy gave Julia the tools and the embodied experience of witnessing her own beauty and power when the world was not able to do so.

Case Study: Nadine

Julia's journey was launched and nourished by the sand and the symbols she used within it. The next client, a seven-year-old whom I shall call Nadine, demonstrated the value of accessing many tools for the resourceful expression of psyche, soul and spirit. She moved with ease from sandplay, to art, to embodied drama and movement, to play, to nature, and then back to sandplay and art. From within an office setting to the wilds of the land and the river's edge, there have been many portals to the deep Self within Nadine's journey.

Nadine began therapy due to low self-esteem that stemmed from a challenging learning disability. Her spectacular imagination was a source of tremendous resiliency but living in the world with all of its demands was at times painful and hard to navigate. A polarity developed in her psychic system whereby her resourceful imaginative play existed alongside an interpersonal rigidity that was becoming more pronounced as she became older. In addition, her ability to process information in the way that schools require meant having to let go of her own unique systems of processing. However, like the shell precariously propped on the vase (see Figure 6.4), the systems Nadine had developed were beautiful but not efficient, which created stress. This unique worldview (including how she found joy and meaning) needed to be seen, witnessed, and nourished as she continued to navigate the demands of the academic world. Like a cool mountain stream, Nadine moved fluidly between varied modalities, eager to find a current that would match her own wild self. She seemed most joyful and in touch with her deepest longings when she could experience freedom and abandon outside the confines of the norm.

Figure 6.4: Shell Precariously Propped on Vase

Nadine came to therapy at a time when her gentle soul was beginning to shut down (in her public life) due to the disconnect between her boundless imagination and the boundaried experiences that are required in school – even in the progressive, creative and nurturing school she attended. For Nadine – Parker Palmer's shy soul metaphor truly resonated:

> The only metaphor I know that reflects the soul's essence while honoring its mystery [is this]: the soul is like a wild animal. Like a wild animal, the soul is tough, resilient, resourceful, savvy, and self-sufficient: it knows how to survive in hard places... Yet despite its toughness, the soul is also shy. Just like a wild animal, it seeks safety in the dense underbrush, especially when other people are around. If we want to see a wild animal, we know that the last thing we should do is go crashing through the woods yelling for it to come out. But if we will walk quietly into the woods, sit patiently at the base of a tree, breathe with the earth, and fade into our surroundings, the wild creature we seek might put in an appearance. We may see it only briefly and only out of the corner of an eye – but the sight is a gift we will always treasure as an end in itself. (Palmer 2004, pp. 58–59)

Creating a safe and loving "field" where the shy soul will venture out to play was exactly what Nadine needed.

It is my belief that there are many paths to source. Identifying which portal is available and receptive to change, healing, and transformation is a wonderful and effective way to work. Change can be accelerated by aligning with the child. To facilitate this, having several tools in the toolbox is extremely helpful as a clinician. Nadine's deep play journey offers a useful lens for multi-modality work. In this brief overview of her journey, I will offer a few highlights of her deep and varied process.

She launched her work by making potions, special brews and balms. Some were contained in a collection of jars but the most dramatic "brew" was contained in a massive three foot diameter cauldron that she brought to her sessions, whose blackness and size was big enough to hold and "showcase" her magical world (Figure 6.5). The dark recesses of this container were a wonderful metaphor for the value of the shadow.

Figure 6.5: Nadine's Cauldron

At the same time as she made the cauldron concoctions, Nadine embarked on a series of sand trays that were focused on establishing a subterranean and sturdy tunnel system in the deep sandbox of play therapist Dennis McCarthy, in whose office I work. The deeper box that sits on the floor invites a sense of full body engagement. Nadine intuitively perceived this invitation on a deep level, crawled into the box one day and sat on a sand mound that she created as if incubating some aspect of Self that needed time to grow. Whatever she was "hatching" needed all of her attention and resources.

Soon after, Nadine began a serious excavation process. The depth of the box (approximately 12 inches or 30 cm) allowed the mining of deep internal topography. As she dug and tunneled on all fours, she inserted tubes to re-enforce and support the emerging infrastructure. It seemed she was "repairing" on a foundational level and her psyche wanting on-going access to the depths as part of her unfolding journey. Week after week, she worked diligently and fully engaged her body, mind, heart, and spirit. Being able to work so deeply encouraged a type of embodied engagement that her psyche and nervous system seemed to crave. Something raw and primal was being accessed and this level of kinesthetic plunge was exactly what was needed. We can't always know or name what is happening, but we can sense when a process is clearly vital.

Nadine's work moved in blocks of creative immersion. After the tunnels were well established and highly functional, she created elaborate multi-tiered water systems where water was gently coaxed from one shell to another in a labyrinthine system of flow. In each of these examples, Nadine persevered in finding resourceful solutions to whatever challenges emerged. She delighted in the complexity yet was never interested in what was expedient. This was a source of strength when it came to the imagination's agenda, but a source of frustration in terms of academic tasks where expedience is a valued and needed skill.

After months of dedicated work and problem solving, she began to spontaneously tear newspapers, creating large mounds of paper. This was "a union of opposites experience" as the spontaneous tearing was the opposite of her careful tunneling and water flow creations. As cited earlier, an encounter with the union of opposites is essential for the individuation process activating the innate drive towards wholeness.

Nadine was at her most joyful when tearing and throwing paper with complete abandon. She would immerse herself in the massive pile and hide and then leap with joy and glee as she flung the paper everywhere. Dennis McCarthy once shared the observation that the act of tearing paper seems to offer the benefit of regulating the nervous system, which certainly seemed to be the case for Nadine. But also critical was her experiencing the sheer freedom that genuine play truly offers. For her this was something not easily accessible in the external world (Figure 6.6).

In Nadine's diverse and joyous encounters with various modalities, her most peaceful and vital self was accessed when she could do her work in nature. There were times we brought paints to the river's edge near my home office, where she soaked her feet in the cool stream while sitting on a rock, painting and humming (Figure 6.6). These were her most unifying experiences and it was helpful to Nadine's growing sense of well-being to have these magical moments not only witnessed but understood and shared for the profound gifts that they offered her.

Figure 6.6: River's Edge

While in nature, Nadine seemed to be completely at home, uniquely herself. Being in direct contact with the power, beauty, and silence of nature and the elements, allowed Nadine to abide in a deep place of rest. Here she truly belonged; here she could disarm and genuinely "be."

Symbolically, water is often viewed as the elemental gateway to the unconscious. From an alchemical perspective, water can symbolize a willingness to allow one's defenses to dissolve (*solutio*), creating more easeful access to the genuine feelings below. Kate Amatruda (1997) links the element of water to the developmental task of attachment and separation in *The Elemental Model*. This model combines the wisdom of the elements with the Tibetan Chakra system and Jungian

Sandplay symbolism. At the water's edge, Nadine was forging and living a new differentiated self, one that was more confident (grounded) and securely attached. As children develop, they need to differentiate and maintain a secure home base so they can find and celebrate their uniqueness without compromising the fundamental source of support in the family.

The wildness of the land spoke to the "wild girl" archetype deep within. Here there were no rules, simply the invitation to be who you are. Sitting at the river's edge, Nadine entered a state of flow, comparable to a peak experience as described by Abraham Maslow. She lost a sense of time, became "unconscious" of self and simply "was" in alignment and in relationship with her surroundings. There was a felt sense of being nourished at the deepest level as if arriving at the "watering hole." Her earlier connections with water (through the potions, the cauldron and the fountains) were more contained; now her connection found its free flowing source, both externally and within.

Due to Nadine's unique and bold creative expressions, she sometimes felt a deep loneliness. It was not easy to fit in and the world was not always receptive to the yearnings of her imagination. But in the safety of the therapeutic space, she found the support and freedom to follow her imaginative whims, no holds barred. She did not have to dilute herself or keep her Self small; she could experience her largeness and have that witnessed and held. This strong therapeutic connection – in collaboration with loving and devoted parents and supportive/ enlightened school administrators and teachers – all converged to help Nadine navigate her public life without compromising the radiance of her inner life. One of her last entries in her Art and Feelings journal which she used in her third grade (UK Year 4) classroom whenever she needed – says it all: "With my art, it is safe to show the real me; my REAL Heart. I miss my real heart; this is the true me" (Figure 6.7). We both paused and breathed together knowing how very precious this beautiful and unique heart is.

Figure 6.7: My True Self

We shared a deep knowing that transcends age and time. We talked for a while about how to remember that beautiful heart when we inevitability forget our intrinsic value; how to let the world see our radiance and aliveness and not hide our beauty and power. While the heart held both the loneliness and the beauty, it was a powerful moment as Nadine got to see it, name it, share it, and catch a glimpse of its true capacity. Making contact with and living with this big heart gave Nadine the courage to engage with the real world with a newly minted sense of confidence and flexibility. While school was still demanding, she found resources within to manage and navigate this stress, while still inhabiting her passions and creativity.

When to terminate

I have found that children intuitively know when they are ready to end therapy and to let go. Whereas they are reluctant to miss even one session when genuinely engaged, they begin to want play dates and to get back to their life when they have completed their developmental tasks and are ready to move on. I am always amazed at how organically termination unfolds, and I have learned to trust the process. Sometimes I, as the clinician, have already arrived at termination's doorstep but I have learned to trust the children; they know when to stop or take a break and I have learned to be patient.

In addition to this intuitive sense of readiness cited above, it is helpful to have some agreed-upon definitions of wellness. This is particularly helpful when talking with parents. Because our field often focuses on symptoms and what is not working, our scope of practice and our understanding of what wellness actually means has been limited. As a profession, we are versed in dis-ease but not so versed in ease.

The work of neuro-scientist and author Daniel Siegel (2007) has been very instructive in articulating *mental health and wellness*. I have used Siegel's work to identify useful barometers indicating when we have arrived at a healthy plateau. In his research, Siegel surveyed all the social sciences to pursue a more universal definition of mental health. To this end, he identified and constructed two acronyms to describe the language of health and integration: COAL and FACES. COAL stands for the state of simultaneous Curiosity, Openness, Acceptance and Love (p.15). But don't be fooled by its simplicity. In fact, I wonder if you could say that a COAL mindset actually stimulates the innate drive towards wholeness? The second acronym – FACES – seeks to articulate the most defining features of wholeness and wellness. Siegel says that *mental health* (emphasis on health) is achieved when thoughts, emotions, and relationships are experienced as Flexible, Adaptive, Coherent, Energized, and Stable. The "C" in FACES is yet another acronym. Siegel defines Coherence as: Connected, Open, Harmonious, Engaged, Receptive, Emergent (something fresh is alive and new), Noetic (deep sense of knowing) Compassionate, and Empathic. We can apply this model to our emotional well-being, our cognitive well-being, our physical well-being and our spiritual well-being. I find these distilled frameworks quite useful. They have helped me articulate the qualities I look for when I intuitively feel ready to terminate.

In closing, deep play can be accessed through many portals, but ultimately it is the core Self that must be engaged for *sustainable change* to occur. Accessing this Self is truly a magical and luminous encounter. Making contact with our most resilient inner core allows for the mysterious process of transformation to manifest and take root. Sharing that encounter and being known in such a deep way creates the energetic field for deep play and deep change. As clinicians, having access to our own inner child and core Self activates a resonance field that accelerates the possibility for change. We become the beacon holders for what is possible. There is an old adage in our field: you can't take clients past where you haven't been yourself. The attuned capacity of the clinician offers a skillful compass for deep engagement and for emotional and spiritual growth and development. This attunement is fundamental to the presence we bring to the work we do.

References

Amatruda, K., & Simpson, P.H. (1997). *Sandplay and the Sacred Healing: A Guide to Symbolic Process*. Novato, California: www.psycheu.com

Andrews, T. (1993) *Animal Speaks: The Spiritual and Magical Powers of Creatures Great and Small*. Woodbury, MN: Llewellyn Press.

Brach, T. (2003) *Radical Acceptance: Embracing your Life with the Heart of a Buddha*. New York, NY: Bantam Dell.

Eason, C. (2007) *Fabulous Creatures, Mythical Monsters, and Animal Power Symbols: A Handbook*. Westport, CT: Greenwood Publishers.

Frost, S. (2010) *Evolving Soulcollage®*. Santa Cruz, CA: Hanford Mead Publishers, Inc.

Graves, R. (1959) Larousse Encyclopedia of Mythology. New York, NY: Batchworth Press.

Jung, C.G., von Franz, M,, Henderson, J.L., Jacobi, J. and Jaffe, A. (1964) *Man and His Symbols*. New York, NY: Dell Publishing Co., Inc.

Jung, C.G. (1973) *Synchronicity: An Acausal Connecting Principle*. Princeton, NJ: Princeton University Press.

Palmer, Parker J. (2004) *A Hidden Wholeness: The Journey Toward an Undivided Life*. San Francisco, CA: Jossey-Bass.

Siegel, Daniel (2007) *The Mindful Brain: Reflection and Attunement in the Cultivation of Well-Being*. New York, NY and London, UK: W.W. Norton and Company.

Sharp, D. (1990) *C.G. Jung Lexicon: A Primer of Terms and Concepts (Studies in Jungian Psychology by Jungian Analysts*. Toronto, ON: Inner City Books.

Some, M.P. (1994) *Of Water and The Spirit: Ritual, Magic and the Initiation of an African Shaman*. Harmondsworth, UK: Penguin Group.

Welwood, J. (1996) *Love and Awakening: Discovering The Path of Intimate Relationship*. New York, NJ: Harper Collins Publishers.

Whitmont, E.C. (1969) *The Symbolic Quest: Basic Concepts of Analytical Psychology*. Princeton, NJ: Princeton University Press.

Weiss, Nancy and Raphael, Jane (2013) *How to Make MeCards4Kids*. Santa Cruz, CA: Handford Mead Publishers, Inc.

Further Reading

Cooper, J.C. (1978). *An Illustrated Encyclopedia of Traditional Symbols.* New York, NY: Thames and Hudson, Inc.

Graves, R. (1959). *Larousse Encyclopedia of Mythology.* New York, NY: Batchworth Press.

Jung, C.G., von Franz, M.L., Henderson, J.L., Jacobi, J., & Jaffe, A. (1964). *Man and His Symbols.* New York, NY: Dell Publishing Co., Inc.

Jung, C.G. (1973). *Synchronicity: An Acausal Connecting Principle.* Princeton, New Jersey: Princeton University Press.

Kalff, D.M. (2003). *Sandplay: A Psychotherapeutic Approach to the Psyche.* Cloverdale, CA: Temenos Press.

Louv, Richard. (2005). *Last Child in the Woods: Saving our Children.* New York, NY: Algonquin Books of Chapel Hill

Moon, Beverly, ed. (1991). *An Encyclopedia of Archetypal Symbolism.* Boston and London, UK: Shambala Press.

Whitmont, E.C. (1969). *The Symbolic Quest: Basic Concepts of Analytical Pyschology.* Princeton, NJ: Princeton University

CHAPTER SEVEN

Deep Sand

Body-centered, Imaginative Play

Dennis McCarthy

Dream: I am leading a group of people to a crossroads in a village. In the center of the crossroads there is a circular well. The well seems to contain tar, like the tar pits in which the bones of ancient creatures are found. We stand around the well and it begins to turn slowly in a clockwise direction. As the well turns a creature slowly emerges from the tar. It is a winged dragon, and a very ancient one at that. It is coming back to life. We stand in awe of it even as I wonder what to do about it.

Upon entering my office, one first sees hundreds of drawings of monsters done by children. They cover every bit of wall space and welcome the whole child into the space. For the most part they are images of what children imagined they would look like if they turned into a monster. They seem to reassure the child entering that this is a safe place in which to play deeply. Like the monsters carved in wood or painted on cloth in Tibetan Buddhist shrine rooms, these monsters drawn by children are potentially "fierce figures on the side of good" (Whyte 1990, p.25). I have never had a child express fear or dismay at these monstrous forms. Even very timid children seem to recognize them as kindred spirits. There is often an element of levity in these monsters that makes their monstrousness more balanced. They offer a small but pure experience of life force, that which we are all blessed with and struggle with from birth until death. They arise from the underworld in the psyche, which in children is not yet separate from the above world.

In the center of this monstrous array is a deep sandbox and next to it a shallow one. The deep box (roughly 28 inches (70 cm) square and 12 inches (30 cm) deep) is the main one used by children. The shallow one is used infrequently, possibly for alternate universes, invading armies or subtexts to the main story the child has created in the deeper box. These subtexts may also be important to the story and to what the child is struggling to rectify in themselves and their lives. But the deep box is the center of play. On occasion, a child who is rigid or insecure about their capacity for imagination may use the shallow box initially. But they all move into the deep box sooner or later without my initiating it. This is where the real action of the therapy occurs, where a potential for direct experience of the psyche exists.

I have long ago understood the efficacy of play and its power to help change children's lives. I am now especially interested in understanding the moments of change that occur in a child's therapy process and the images and play experiences that trigger or accompany these moments. I am also interested in understanding the point at which change can occur, when the ground is now fertile for new seeds to grow in the child. It's important to remember that these seeds exist in the child already. It is our job and our privilege to help the fertilizing, germinating process.

I would like to focus in this chapter on several of these moments of change, in which a child stood up from an experience of sandplay and was not the same child who had knelt down by the box. Their defense system had reorganized, becoming more functional and less rigid. Or perhaps a deep wound from trauma had healed, or their perception of self or their world had altered. To identify these moments may teach us a great deal about the inner life of the child as well as the art of psychotherapy itself. That these moments happened as part of a sequence of play is of course true. That they may have been aided by shifts at home with their parents or changes in school placement is also true. But there is often a moment of transformation in play therapy that is imbued with life force awakened, resurrected or renewed, and it is these numinous moments that I want to focus on.

It is first necessary to consider why the use of a deep sandbox is so important. I have heard varying theories as to why most psychotherapists who use sandplay with children use a shallow box. None of these make any sense to me. A shallow box lacks the sense of the vertical, the experience of descent and ascent that is so necessary for psychic change. The shallow box lacks the ability for things to sink out of sight or rise up from below, both important in therapeutic play. It diminishes greatly the necessary stage of deconstructive play that children go through; when things fall apart, when worlds are depicted as blowing up or caving in, when the underworld and the above world meet or even switch places for a time. The necessity of making a mess is inhibited by the shallow box, which may be one unconscious reason for its use. The type of play the deep box encourages is not neat and tidy. And equally important, the deep box allows for the experience of *grounding*, which is a central tenet in my work with children. It is not that the shallow box has no value but its limitations and the rigidity with which its adherents defend it are of concern. The shallow box may satisfy an adult who is using it to express in images what can't be expressed in words or to explore consciously certain emotionally charged images. Children too will use a shallow box or no box at all to express themselves when truly engaged in the process. This is the nature of play. But the deep box offers the moving child a chance to be moved by their play in a much deeper way. I cannot stress this enough.

Sandplay was first developed as a therapeutic form prior to the awareness of the body's centrality in true psychotherapeutic process. Psychology still saw the body as separate from the mind, and if anything an encumbrance to it. In the overly intellectualized world of the analyst's couch, the body was not an ally in the process but the source of sexual fantasies and other id-driven impulses that needed to be resolved. There was still a great deal of repression and rigidity in psychology when sandplay was being conceptualized, which thinkers such as Wilhelm Reich, Alexander Lowen and others rebelled against. Wilhelm Reich's work embraced the body and sexuality, but his approach was seen as too radical by most. He believed that the function of treatment should be the re-establishment of the natural capacity for love. This still seems like it should be a goal in all of our therapeutic efforts. Alexander Lowen (1990) furthered Reich's ideas in his bioenergetic approach to psychotherapy, stressing the body as the core of his analytic work, and the capacity or pleasure as a key goal. He contributed invaluable ideas about self-assertion and self-awareness (see his book *Pleasure*) that figure greatly in my own approach to play therapy.

Reich and Lowen undervalued the imagination in their eagerness to get psychotherapy out of the head, creating imbalance in another direction. But they encouraged us to be sexual, to have powerful emotions and to feel pleasure. They brought flesh and bones and breath into psychotherapy and for that alone we owe them a great debt. They introduced the concept of *energy* into western thinking. The work of dance therapists, and other body-centered therapists, along with these two theorists has helped bring the body into the process of psychotherapy.

We now know that we are not "talking heads." We are our musculature, our breath, our viscera, our neurology. We are the instinctual impulses that define us as alive and human. These basic impulses are now seen as positive and essential by many in the field of psychotherapy. To ignore the body or not to accommodate its expression in working with children especially is to miss the essence of the child. Children still live fully in their bodies or are struggling to do so, even if these bodies are dysregulated, ungrounded, or have been mistreated. The symbols that arise in their play arise as much from body as from psyche. In fact the two have not yet been severed in the child, although the one may be beginning to be pitted against the other. It is our job then to reunite them in play. And it is the child's natural impulse to do so.

It was deemed possible in the old schemas of child psychotherapy to effect change just by getting children to speak directly about their lives or through the use of symbols, especially archetypal ones. But words are not the child's primary language and without being grounded in the reality of the body, the symbol's power may go unused in the child's life. In symbolic play in the deep box, the energy in the symbols often manifests then and there. We can see the act of accessing it and its integration into the child's being right before us. Images that are not traditionally seen as archetypal may act with archetypal urgency and power. It is not we as psychotherapists who get to decide what images should have meaning for the child but rather the child who uses or produces them in their play. We get to witness, help provoke, and participate in the act of transformation, if we are lucky.

In recent years, a simple ball of clay, a plastic tank, and an empty bowl have all been vehicles of deep change because a child imbued them with deep meaning, with life force. For a moment these simple objects were living matter or brought this living matter into being: they mattered. In the deeper box many images can become infused with life force, tapping into archetypal energy. The child may bring the world they have made to life and, in animating it and altering it, be altered as well.

My own use of sandplay began without any awareness that a method of therapy called sandplay had been developed by Dora Kalff several years prior. I simply included a sandbox in my first play therapy space since it made sense to do so. I recalled playing in such a box as a child. Initially the box I used was quite large so the child could sit in it as well as play by it. Each time I made a new box I made it slightly smaller but just as deep, noticing that its use increased and deepened as its size decreased.

Having spent almost forty years watching children play in a deep box and engaging with them in the experience, I can definitely say that the deep box is a much more visceral, emotional, and energy laden experience. When the child kneels down by the deep box, and digs their hands into the sand, there is an almost immediate, visible physical response. It may be subtle or it may be overt. They may sweat, pant, pass gas, and even drool. Their faces may become flushed and they often have to run to the bathroom. This physical excitation is obvious and transformative. I suspect that this might frighten and even offend many therapists. It may seem regressive, but that is part of what makes it healing: regression in the service of the ego in the context of a therapeutic relationship in a safe space equals growth.

Before we descend into case material I want to offer three ideas about regulation that describe the levels of engagement that are possible with the child in a deep sand experience. The first is by neuroscientist Antonio Damasio from his book *The Feeling of What Happens – Body and Emotion in the Making of Consciousness* (1999). In referring to "The Levels of Life Regulation," he places the biological states or drives at the bottom. Above these drives are emotions and above emotions are feelings (sensory patterns). At the top, in the realm of consciousness, he places "high reason." He is describing the biological role our physiology and emotions play in becoming conscious. Movement can occur from the bottom up or vice versa. (Damasio 1999, p.55). Alexander Lowen, in his book *The Spirituality of the Body* (1990), has a similar table that he calls "The Hierarchy of the Personality." In this pyramid-shaped table he places the energetic processes that activate us at the bottom. These processes result in movements that lead to feelings that become thoughts (Lowen 1990, p.24). Ann Ulanov cites Winnicott in her book *Finding Space – Winnicott, God and Psychic Reality* in which Winnicott is basically saying the same thing when he talks about aggression. "Aggression starts by showing itself as energy – crude, uninhibited, bubbling up from the body – to be housed by each of us. Such dynamic animation leads to movement and then to exploration of the environment" (Ulanov 2001, p.107). These three theorists are describing the biological forces at play that give rise to consciousness, help in forming connections with others, leading potentially to a unified sense of self.

The validity of these ideas is evidenced by children in play therapy. Children have not yet lost this connection to body, with its instinct driven energy and bubbling creative and aggressive life force. There is an immediacy in their ability to access emotions and impulses, which when thwarted can become anxiety, depression, or negative impulsivity. They don't need to talk about these emotions and impulses but to express them in a safe and satisfying way. The "direct experience" of life that Zen Buddhists and others speak of is how children still live, especially if they are allowed to move freely.

My goal is always to try and help the child not be afraid of themselves, of that which lives within them. This is true no matter what the presenting problem is. This statement of purpose dictates the materials and techniques I offer children and their use, as well as how I conceptualize what needs to happen. Ideally, if dysregulated children learn to ground their energy and express themselves in ways that more fully satisfy them, their defense system will change and they will become more regulated. The dysregulated and self-negating energy may turn into creativity. If suppressed children can turn their aggression outwards in a playful way they may come to truly love and value themselves. The very force that was causing them pain can become one that brings pleasure. It is important to accept that most children do want to function better, be social, and express and experience love of life and self and other.

Case Study: Cara

Nine-year-old Cara sat by the deep box, digging into its depth and clearly experiencing this depth in herself. I sensed the weariness in this girl as she played. She lived with a troubled older brother, a very self-centered father and a mother overwhelmed by the effort to try to fix everything and make everyone happy. Cara, in attempting to mollify her family and not be an added burden, as well as being the peacemaker in her school placement, found there was little room for her own needs. She had never really gone through "the terrible twos" as there seemed no room for this with her brother and father taking up so much space. She had always been pleasant, undemanding, and attuned to the needs of others. The latter was a gift of hers but in the state of suppressed aggression/expression she was in it had hobbled her. She was proud of her popularity in school but I sensed that it took much effort to sustain this. When she sat creating this particular world in the sand with me, her brother was finally getting help, her parents had separated and she was now in a position to make more room for herself, to take up more space.

She made and then unmade a land of mountains, rivers, and waterfalls. When she was done with the excavating aspect of her play what remained was one large mountain in the boxes' center with four smaller mountains in each corner. On each of the corner mountains stood a female figure. In the center was a fierce king. The four women circling him were busy trying to placate him by dancing and singing. But they had to keep doing this continually like Scheherazade in the Arabian tale. If they stopped placating him he would destroy them and their world.

After contemplating this dilemma, I asked her if there wasn't some other way forward for these women aside from eternally entertaining an evil king. Surely there must be a more effective way of dealing with him. She considered this for quite some time and then had me close my eyes while she made some adjustments. Upon opening my eyes the sand didn't look any different but the girl did. She looked enlivened by whatever she had just done. In bringing the world she had made to life, it was revealed that she had buried canons and other large guns in front of each female facing the king. These slowly and dramatically rose up from below. Suddenly the king got nervous and left, replaced by a benevolent and powerful queen (whose name happened to be the same as this child's).

When the queen showed up the whole world changed. Steps were added from the small mountains to the central one, allowing easy access to and for her. The females standing guard left their perches and came to be with the queen. Numerous gems and flowers were added, as well as wild horses running in the valley below. This girl, the new queen's namesake, looked and felt very different simply by placing the guns in the sand, knowing they would emerge. Their emerging was not tenuous. The aggression and self-assertion they described arose in her consciousness as the weapons rose up. The females in the sand were no longer holding things together but solving the problem. No one had been slain, just an assertion of "no" had been depicted without words. It is hard to describe in words the potency of this simple gesture.

Later in that same session, she made her brother out of clay and happily demolished him with a rubber mallet again and again. She used her whole body to do this. She carved "rest in peace" on the smeared remains. There was no horror in this cathartic play. She was simply externalizing further the emotions that had been turned on herself. She assured me (and herself) that she loved her brother but enough was enough. When she stood up from demolishing she stood taller and more sure-footed. She was beginning to know who she was. The act of arming the girls in the sand had changed her defense system.

In Cara's next session she made a central mountain on which the same four female figures stood surrounding their queen, with their canons in front of them, ready for action. They were singing and dancing still but now it was for them to enjoy: self-expression as opposed to defensiveness. The same actions became celebratory of self. By her third scene a few weeks later the guns were gone and the women just were, free and at peace. Meanwhile Cara's mother reported that her daughter had been saying "no" frequently at home and that it was so much like the "no" of a toddler that at times both of them would burst out laughing. But the "no" did its job despite the levity. She acted and seemed more solid, more herself. We would spend subsequent sessions reinforcing this change, as well as helping her parents tolerate and even appreciate a more assertive child at home.

Again, deeper sand creates an easier and often immediate connection to the child's physiology, including their musculature, their nervous system and their viscera. This has the ability to affect metabolism, brain chemistry, and the personality that arise out of our body self. It has the capacity to detoxify, to rid the child of that which is living in them that is anti-self. This doesn't always happen of course and when it doesn't I often don't know why it hasn't. I also don't always know why it has when it has. But in cases such as this we can see change happening before our very eyes and it is both awesome and matter of fact.

I have never worked with a child whose growth and maturation I was able to see and participate in who changed without the manifestation of aggression in their play. Aggression is a life force, inherent and central to emotional development and contributing to our discovery of the world around us. Interference in its expression compromises psychic maturation. Cara aggressed easily when her life situation was ready to accommodate this, when she was supported in its expression by play that allowed for it, and in a relationship that could tolerate and understand its necessity. Her family benefited too from her shift in her defense system as it rippled through all of her relationships, provoking change in them as well.

Case Study: Gabriel

Many children rarely use the sand at all, but in some cases the one time they do so may be a pivotal one. Gabriel, a five-year-old boy who had been sexually abused by his mother and her boyfriend when he was three was being forced by the courts to have weekly supervised visits with her when I began seeing him. He lived in a secure environment with his paternal grandparents and father but this was disrupted by these weekly visits that stirred up the early trauma. Even in the security of his father's home he lived in a fairly dissociative state, and the visits made healing impossible. His father was trying desperately to have these visits stopped. But until they could be ended, I urged his father to stop at a river they passed on their way home from these visits to throw stones into it with his son. Doing this helped in some small way to dispel the pall the visits had on both the boy and his father. Meanwhile the boy came to play.

He avoided the sand for the first six months of treatment, except to sometimes throw something into it from afar. These gestures felt emotionally laden but he was not ready or willing to do more. In his early sessions with me he was fairly dissociated. He would wander off in the middle of play or check to see that his father was still in the waiting room, his eyes glazed over, his body still manifesting the memory of abuse in its disjointedness and tension. When he did settle into play it was always cathartic in nature. He used a small guillotine to decapitate a zombie, whose head he would then try to reconnect to its body. The boy shrieked with terror as the head came close to its body. He would then use a rubber mallet to pound the head flat laughing with delight. The boy's body actually trembled with fear as he watched the head seek its body. The emotional shift from terror to delight was quite potent. He repeated this dozens and dozens of times over the course of the next few weeks.

In the midst of all of his play he would climb onto a large ball I have in my office and pretend it was a school bus. My job was to hold him secure as he walked on the ball and moved it through the space. This simple play activity, which he experienced with hilarity, required that I hold him securely and yet allow him to move. I had to be grounded and ground him in the midst of upheaval.

He then instructed me to build a large monster out of clay with openings at the mouth, the genitals, and the anus, all linked. He created "potions" using watercolor paints and fed them to the monster, with the potions spurting out of both openings. He shouted with delight as he repeated this again and again in numerous sessions. There was always a shiver of energy that would course through him each time that he did it, indicating the powerful effect it was having on him physiologically and emotionally. This action was both a poisoning and a detox, a paradoxical remedy of his own invention. Both of us would get soaked by the monster's messy flooding, especially me. This flooding felt like an intentional and significant part of the play. This play too went on for many weeks. At one point the boy had me make an eye in the monster's forehead so that the water might go up and emerge from this "third eye" as well. The monster had to be very flooded to allow for this ascending flow of water. Yet when it worked the monster began to seem like an enlightened being! During this period his mother had lapsed into drug addiction and he didn't see her for almost a year. This created an uninterrupted positive holding environment at home and allowed his work with me to be truly therapeutic.

In one session that felt like a crescendo of all his many months of flooding, he pummeled the monster afterwards until it was flat. He seemed to be done with it. He even apologized for getting me wet, a sign of some new consciousness creeping in. Then he went to the sand and he created the following scene, his first, in the deep box:

> There is a pool in a deep valley with no water in it. Several children are in the pool along with several ghosts. The ghosts are menacing the children. A group of army men come and surround the pool and then fill it with water. The children are freed by this flooding but the ghosts become stuck. Once the children are out of danger the army men cover the ghosts with a mountain of sand and then pound it down to make sure that the ghosts are dead.

In the shallow box next to this he then created the following scene:

> The same army men are now guarding an enormous amount of treasure. Some of the treasure is hidden under large clamshells but much of it is in plain sight. There is no chance of the treasure being stolen as it is secure in their care. The army men take shifts so that they have time to sleep as well.

The scene in the deep box was an amazing reiteration of what had happened inwardly for him. And it addresses the fear of flooding that so many therapists worry about with children. For this boy flooding saved the children. The many months of flooding the clay monster had helped to manifest the deep sand story, in which flooding freed the children and trapped the ghosts. The accompanying scene in which there was a mixture of vigilance and rest, of buried and exposed treasure, seemed to both convey and to create a further shift in his defense system.

When I next saw this boy, a few weeks later, he greeted me with open arms. "I've missed you!" he cried, "It's been so long since I saw you!" It had not been that long but it was certainly a new boy who greeted me. He now moved in an integrated manner, and his body seemed relaxed. And for the first time he played naturally, exploring the various possibilities in the space as if seeing many of them for the first time.

Tolerating repetitive play such as this child's can be difficult. We may not know where it will lead or when to help the child move on. Erik Erikson referred to repetitive play as "traumatic" play that is often resolved by cathartic play (Erikson 1977, p.42). This boy's zombie beheadings and his monster detoxification were both repetitive and cathartic, whereas his deep scene was a cathartic resolution of the problem.

One fear that many therapists have of the deeper sandbox may be the sense of "flooding" that it affords. Even wet sand is something one is cautioned against by many as it may cause regression. I welcome regression as it leads to deep change. For this boy, who felt flooded with feelings, his play needed to replicate and then discharge his emotions that were too much for him to feel let alone talk about. And I needed to tolerate this as well getting soaked myself in the process. There was no other way forward.

More moments of deep change

A ten-year-old boy entered treatment with a knife phobia. He was suddenly afraid he might stab himself with a knife and the knives in the kitchen had to be hidden from him. He was riddled with anxiety about this, which was interfering with all aspects of his life. Meanwhile he still slept in the same bed with his deeply embattled parents. They fought viciously and frequently within earshot of him and meanwhile lectured him on ethics. He had never told them to stop and never asserted his individuality with them. He was a perfectionist, albeit a successful one. He had numerous friends and was a star student and athlete as well. But the knife emerged as a potent symbol that unnerved him and his parents and required that they all change. It was a symbol that was both symptom and cure.

He spent weeks playing aggressively with me, embodying the energy of the knife in his play with me but avoiding the sand. I spent weeks helping his parents to battle more effectively without their son present and to tolerate their son's efforts at self-assertion as well as letting him sleep in his own bed. They entered couples therapy and began a process of deep change. With my support they tolerated a more outspoken son. His knife phobia was soon gone and he and his parents felt better. But I was convinced that something had not yet occurred in his play, some piece of imaginative work. And he had yet to play in the sand. So I offered the child a small "gem", a plastic ruby, if he would make a world in the sand. He liked the challenge as much as the reward and he made the following world:

> In a deep valley on the moon a hero, who is an astronaut, marches along protected by a group of soldiers. On the hills surrounding them there are several monsters waiting who pounce on the hero and his guards and destroy them. The dead bodies are flung to one side.

I was both disturbed and annoyed by this scene. It was done with a smug indifference, a precociousness that flew in the face of his only having recently been able to sleep on his own. He seemed afraid to play imaginatively. So I asked him to try again. He repeated the same scene with the same results a few more times. I challenged him to find another ending to the story. Then he changed things.

> The hero, now "a brave knight," walks the same path but this time his guards are animals. A wolf, a lion, an eagle, and a Tiger walk beside him. They sense the presence of monsters on the surrounding hills, and they attack them before the monsters can attack the hero. The monsters are killed. All the earlier slain heroes and guards are resurrected.

The boy stood up from this sand world and his body shook in one long rippling spasm from his toes to head, much like a dog. It was one huge shiver. Then he said in amazement "I feel different now!" And he was.

Case Study: Making the upside down world right

A twelve-year-old boy struggling with anorexia battled with me furiously for several months using foam encounter bats while he battled with his mother at home not to eat. The level of intensity to his fighting with me was amazing, yet he never hurt me. He would enter my office sullen and withdrawn and leave smiling and flushed. He seemed furious when he fought and had many reasons to be so. He had been caught in the middle of his parent's ugly marriage and even uglier divorce. He allowed me to talk with him about these issues in his family over time, which softened his fury into tears of grief. But he stayed stuck in the anorexic impasse.

In his first session he'd made a world in the sand in which everything was upside down. What a disturbing and yet fitting image for a boy who was starving himself at an age when most boys are ravenous. I asked him what could remedy the upside down world and he thought for some time and then added a unicorn on the outer edge of the world. In mythology, the unicorn's horn did in fact have great healing power and so potent was it with phallic power that it continued to sweat even after it was severed from the animal. This pubescent age boy, who was at war with his own body, his own instinct for survival, badly needed the power of that horn. His next sand world, made several weeks later, depicted the world under attack by monsters that had risen up from deep below to punish humans for taking such bad care of the earth. This seemed like a fitting depiction of the anorexic bind:

the body's defense system turned on itself. Versions of this scenario of the natural world's fury at mankind, were repeated several times in the coming weeks.

In the midst of working with this boy I read a book entitled *Dreams of Totality – Where We Are When There's Nothing at the Center* in which the author says "emotions like fury aim to correct by breaking down defensive structures until only the bones of identity remain, bones around which something new can form" (Salman 2013, p.162). This healing aspect of fury has been evident in many of the traumatized children I have worked with, especially so when it can be expressed in the context of a safe play relationship. For this boy, the fury expressed in his battling me and in his deep sand scenes did eventually lead to healing.

After many, many sessions that alternated between him fighting me and sitting in impassive resistance, he returned to the deep box. He made a world in which two men shared tea in a cave far below their village. Before them was "a great treasure" (Figure 7.1).

I was both amazed and deeply moved by this world. After so many months of his furious battling, there was a surprising tenderness in its depiction of the two men having tea. The treasure that they looked upon as they sat was placed with reverence. Upon leaving that day he told his mother he was starving! After this, despite several episodes of regression, he did really begin to master his eating disorder.

Figure 7.1: Finding the Treasure

Case Study: Becoming the mountain

A six-year-old with a serious medical condition lived in a constant state of worry about when he would next be sick, and was frequently in a state of infantile fury at his parents, especially his mother. They in turn were nervous wrecks and had developed their own illnesses that were seen as stress-induced. The boy came to play and in his first visit engaged mainly in chaotic acts of aggression, which I mirrored and attempted to channel and ground. By the session's end he had climbed into my sandbox (he was small enough to fit in it) and had me make a world with him in it. He was immensely happy as he sat half buried in sand and posing as a mountain in the world he had me make around and on him. His mother was amazed to see him so when she came in at session's end. As he explored more forms of grounded aggression with me in the following weeks he emerged from the sand and sat by the box instead. Bouts of illness would bring about a regression in his functioning and his play but he quickly began to move forward again by entering the box and becoming one with the land again. It did not cure his illness but it helped him deal better with some of its incapacitating aspects. And his parent's illnesses disappeared, as he learned to aggress rather than regress. This again brings up the already mentioned and central issue of grounding.

Grounding

Grounding refers to the process of establishing a firm physical and emotional contact with reality. In somatic terms, this means achieving a solid sense of having one's feet on the ground and of being fully in one's body. Gaining the capacity to tolerate the increased excitement that goes with greater personal energy is part of the process of healthy growth. The energy of life must be grounded if it is to be used productively. Play offers the growing child numerous means of achieving this sense of being grounded, which allows for self-regulation and self-possession. Most children who enter treatment are struggling with either a dysregulated or thwarted life force. There may be many causes for this but the approach is the same; that of offering play materials and a process that supports and encourages embodiment as well as the containment and connectedness to self and other that allows for it. The grounded child will move towards health. The ungrounded child will struggle to do so.

Play is by its very nature a grounding experience. Erik Erikson cites Plato in his book *Toys and Reasons* in seeing the model of true playfulness in the need of all young creatures to leap. "To truly leap you must learn how to use the ground as a springboard, and how to land resiliently and safely. It means to test the leeway allowed by given limits, to outdo and yet not escape gravity" (Erikson 1977, p.17). Erikson and Plato are describing grounding. The child in treatment may struggle against obstacles in their psyche, their families and/or their neurology that make leaping and the concomitant groundedness it allows for difficult to achieve. But they also have a greater urgency to do so. This intensified need works in the child's favor in the right relationship and the right play process. This is important to understand in attempting to help troubled children. The buried or thwarted aliveness in the child wants to be reached, wants to surface, wants to be regulated. If we speak to this in the play we offer the child will reply, not in words but in movement, in images, in play.

As I was working on this chapter I was also preparing for a training workshop in play therapy entitled "Harnessing the Dragon." In the midst of thinking and imagining about this training, I had the following experience with an eight-year-old boy I was seeing.

Case Study: Daniel

Daniel had been diagnosed as dyslexic and this not only impacted his ability to read but his speech as well. He moved in a disjointed manner and had the perfectionism and self-consciousness that I have often come to associate with dyslexia. He had been referred to me by a physical therapist he was seeing who he had kicked in the midst of one of her sessions with him. This surprised her in this otherwise passive and cooperative child. She felt there was buried aggression in this act that needed help being expressed and integrated. She was sure this would address the impasse he was at in the remedial reading work he was receiving as well as the sensory work she was doing with him. She described him as being greatly disorganized in his body.

Daniel had two loving parents but his father was away a great deal. When he was out of town, Daniel slept with his mother and this created resentment in him towards his father. His mother was becoming uncomfortable with her son's interest in her body that was feeling sexual to her, as well as increasingly negative comments he was making about his father. This motivated her to help him stay in his own bed at night, with support and encouragement from me. He mastered this easily once she was ready to let him do so.

Meanwhile Daniel came to play. His early play involved creating worlds in both the deep and the shallow boxes. These worlds were really lovely but he was more concerned with their being perfectly constructed than in the story they depicted. There was no potential in them for movement or action. Meanwhile I engaged Daniel in aggressive play using clay. Initially he was angry at my offering him the use of a small guillotine. "How rude!" he said. So he made me out of clay and beheaded me in order to punish me. This made him very happy and he decided to explore more aggressive play with clay. He quickly came to love the idea of each of us making monsters out of clay and battling each other. His monster was always disproportionately large which made him even happier. Our monsters stood in a makeshift boxing ring and at the sound of me ringing a bell we would both leap into the fight. Daniel's body leapt up as his monsters did. After each round our monsters regrouped in their corners. Daniel's monsters got bigger and bigger as each new round ensued. Eventually he grabbed a rubber mallet and pummeled my fighter with great joy. In the midst of one such fight he began to sing the chorus from an old Tears for Fears song; "Shout, shout let it all out!" As he sang these lines he began to shout at the top of his lungs, amazing himself (as well as his mother, who heard him in the waiting room; she assured me later that her son had never shouted before). This shouting felt like an eruption from within, some new vital energy surfacing.

While these battles escalated Daniel's sand worlds did as well. The deep box quickly became filled with scenes that soon dissolved into chaos. In the shallow box he made a very orderly world within the confines of a castle that he assembled each time. These too began to have a feeling of life force and movement. In fact the castle grew in size each week from a small confined area to a vast one. This slow expansion in the shallow box felt as important as the disorganizing play in the deeper box. Then Daniel's scenes grew in number and expanded out of the boxes into the playroom. In one session he made five worlds, each taking place in a different time but all interconnected in the history of the story being told in each. Some were in the sandboxes and some were at various places in the playroom. The expansion of consciousness depicted in the complex relationship the various worlds had to each other was quite moving to witness. Periodically he would once again make a series of very tidy worlds that were beautiful but lacking in life force. I would wonder if he had slipped back into his old pattern, but at sessions end he would make a storm come and destroy his creations with great joy. I have a small "thunder machine" which is a simple cylinder with a spring at one end that does indeed make a sound exactly like thunder. He would attack each box with this, dragging the spring through the lands depicted like the funnel of a tornado and destroy the worlds he had made in them. Watching him playing the role of Poseidon or Shiva, I realized how different he held himself now, how grounded he seemed. This non-attachment to form served him well in his everyday life, where both his reading and his speech improved. It was obvious that as his own consciousness was expanding, so were his cognitive abilities. His parents described a much more assertive child at home.

In one of his final sessions, Daniel made another assortment of worlds that spanned both boxes as well several other boxes I have in another room for training purposes. In the center of all these worlds he made a scene on a large blue sheet of paper representing the sea. An island was constructed in the center, with a small boy, a cave and a tree on it. Then he told the following story:

> On a small island lived a boy sitting on a rock near a tree. A tiny dragon ran by him and fell into the sea. From the depths of the sea it spat acid at the tree, and the tree became a huge seven-headed dragon. This dragon was a good one. Years later the boy fell into the sea and was chased by an evil dragon. He swam very fast away from it. Then a battle ensued between the seven-headed good dragon and the evil one. They fell to the bottom of the sea and arose several times in their fighting. Eventually the evil dragon gave up and left. Years later the boy leapt onto the good dragon's back. They now belonged to each other. (Figure 7.2)

Daniel's description of the dragon's battle sinking and rising conveyed a feeling of powerful change, in the wake of many experiences of mini-changes. When the boy leapt onto the dragon's back to claim his connection with him there was a sense of deep inner connection occurring simultaneously. The puzzle pieces fell into place. The child and the space and the play and my own senses were all humming with aliveness. It was a very big feeling, and yet it was not. Upon his father entering the space at session's end Daniel said simply "let's go!" and out the door he went in a flash.

Figure 7.2: Harnessing the Dragon

In his next visit many weeks later Daniel entered the play space as if he had just left a moment before and made seven worlds spread out through two rooms. Many of the worlds had dragons at the center of them. The world in the deeper box, which seemed to hold the most charge for him, depicted three men digging into the mountainside for treasure. Daniel told me simply "they are going much deeper now to get more treasure" (Figure 7.3). So the journey continues.

Figure 7.3: Going Deeper Now...

Dragons

The dragon is the spirit of nature and the nature of spirit. It is an external form of an internal process. (Huxley 1979) It is life force personified and all five instinctual urges combined: aggression, hunger, sexuality, creativity, and spirituality. Dragons are usually a catalyst for change in their use by children, solving an impasse, although not always in such a nice way. They may be seen as a symbol of necessary revolution, the birth of a new order. Children stand in awe of the dragon image, even when it is they who have chosen or created it. The dragon is both fantastic and terrifying, wonderful and hideous, familiar and mysterious – very much like life itself.

It is important not to become too attached to the images that children create in their play. They are awesome but not precious. The deep sandbox and the enlivened therapeutic relationship allow for moments of profound self-expression and the change inherent in these. The images that emerge and are emissaries of change are tools of expression and experience. What matters most is what these images free up in the child, how they help the child to live in their own skin more fully, in their own families more connectedly, and in their own inner lives, more deeply. What matters most is that they help the child become more capable of giving and receiving love.

Note

All names in the cases have been changed, as well as any information that would render them recognizable. That said, I have worked with thousands of children in my 40 years of practice with many similar symptoms and life situations. I have not altered any relevant details of the child's play, however.

References

Damasio, A. (1999) *The Feeling of What Happens: Body and Emotion in the Making of Consciousness*. New York, NY: Harcourt, Inc.

Erikson, E. (1977) *Toys and Reasons*. New York, NY: Norton.

Huxley L. (1979) *The Dragon*. London, UK: Thames and Hudson.

Lowen, Alexander (1970) *Pleasure*. New York, NY: Penguin.

Lowen, A. (1990) *The Spirituality of the Body*. Basingstoke and New York, NY: Macmillan.

Kalff, D.M. (2003) *Sandplay: A Psychotherapeutic Approach to the Psyche*. Cloverdale, CA: Temenos Press.

Reich, Wilhelm (1986) *The Function of the Orgasm*. New York NY: Farrar Strauss and Giroux.

Salman, S. (2013) *Dreams of Totality – Where We Are When There's Nothing at the Center*. New Orleans, LA: Spring Journal Books.

Ulanov, A. (2001) *Finding Space – Winnicott, God and Psychic Reality*. Louisville, KY: Westminster John Knox Press.

Whyte, D. (1990) *Where Many Rivers Meet*. Langley, WA: Many Rivers Press.

CHAPTER EIGHT

Emergence

A Tale of Two Boys

Neal Brodsky

When a child is brought into the therapy room he is often the standard bearer for a family lineage in need of healing. Whether the young person's diagnosis is related to anxiety, attention deficit, addictive, or oppositional behavior, or family difficulties, we are called as therapists to "go deeper" in helping our clients face and experience what it means to assert their authentic selves while maintaining flexibility as growing humans in a shifting and uncertain world.

The interweaving of body-centered expressive movement, sand, clay, poetry, drawing, and dreams comprises the canvas on which I work with children and adolescents. This chapter focuses on two cases where a combination of body-centered Core Energetics[1] including expressive arts and sandplay allowed two boys to find their own channels for concrete achievement and growing independence in the context of complex and often challenging family lives. Treated

---

1 *Core Energetics*, founded and pioneered by John C. Pierrakos, M.D. blends body psychotherapy with spiritual development. As children, we begin to armor against emotional wounds through chronic "holding" in the musculature and development of a "mask" persona. Core Energetics (see Pierrakos 1987) practice includes physical and consciousness-building activities which seek to restore each person's "Center of Right Energy" (Core), opening the heart to a wider range of emotional response and authentic life expression. Neal Brodsky and colleagues are adapting this work for use with children and adolescents.

separately, they shared me as their therapist and became, through their concurrent process, instruments of each other's healing.

Case Study: Victor, age 13

Victor's parents had heard me speak at a New York City venue on the topic "Finding the Lost Boys" which focused on the challenge of raising sons in today's electronically mediated world where children are often influenced more by peer groups than by authority within their own family. As described by his father, the boy had a complex history. First, both Victor and his 19-year-old brother had been adopted at an early age. Little was known of Victor's birth parents' background except that he was born in one of the former Eastern bloc countries. Victor's adoptive father was an adult child of Jewish Holocaust survivors and his adoptive mother's parents were Catholic. Along with his parents and older brother, Victor had spent the last three years in Europe where his mother had been on assignment. Recently returned to the US, he was now struggling to find a peer group in which he could thrive. Blond, blue eyed, and tall, his parents spoke to me of their worry and his, as to "where Victor fit" among his multi-cultural classmates at the public middle school he was now attending in New York City. In addition, Victor was taking medication for attention deficit issues, first diagnosed when he was eight, several years after his father had gone through a life-threatening bout of cancer from which he was now in remission.

The boy's biggest trouble at school and at home when attempting to do his work, was the ability to settle himself and resist the temptation to play video games on his cell phone. He also struggled to distill the thoughts of his highly creative mind into the written word. From early separate sessions with the boy's father and mother, I was able to gather additional information about the family including intimations of conflict between the parents. Victor had recently been following the family cat into his parent's bed at night and sleeping there instead of in his own room, a childhood habit that had re-surfaced when Victor's older brother, with whom he'd been close, had been taken away to a rehabilitation center for alcohol abuse.

At his first session, Victor was already testing the capacity (and porosity) of the shallow sand tray I'd inherited years earlier from a veteran sandplay therapist and he was also testing me. Upon first learning he could add water to worlds he was creating in the box,

Victor immediately began experimenting with just how much liquid the shallow box would hold, toting plastic container after container and dumping it in, watching the water seep quickly through the sand and eventually through the box seams onto the floor.

With the time near to its end at his first session, he ignored my request for him to wash up, balancing a metal bucket filled with water on two flimsy branches I had brought in from the woods bordering my home in Connecticut. Amazingly, the bucket held, perched precariously in the center of the box above a single golden human figure, flanked by two distinct riverbeds Victor had created with his water play in the sand.

As is my practice when a case calls for it, I reached out for supervision before Victor's next session. My supervisor Dennis McCarthy spoke of the "blurred boundaries" in the family, describing the "family bed" that was created by Victor's night time wanderings as "the soup" of the family. I thought then of the suppressed memory and trauma of the father's cancer, of the pain of familial infertility that often precedes adoption and the desire, as Dennis put it, "to liquefy the multiple layers of flooding that the boy was experiencing," which included his own emotions and reactions to his brother's alcohol abuse. What of Victor's single golden figure in his first sand tray? Dennis said this was akin to numerous creation myths – "a golden individual creating a mythic environment." What might Victor's personal and family "environment" look like if he were to design it? On a practical level, he was about to move into a larger apartment with his parents and had asked me whether I would tell his parents that he wanted to have a "man cave" there – his own special place.

Demonstrating his need for space, Victor began to work in unique ways "above" the shallow box, first using his imagination to "expand the container" in which he was creating. Placing a Buddha-figure in the box, he told me that its powers to stop any possible invading force "went up to the ceiling." He then manifested this "power" by reflecting light as high as the ceiling through a magnifying glass, through crystals and plastic "diamonds" balanced on the top edges of the shallow box and sticking up from half-buried places in the sand. Victor was creatively reaching beyond the borders of the box I had, calling out for even greater depth in which to construct his worlds. Maybe I could help him by providing more material and depth for his multi-dimensional canvas. Dennis urged me to do just this – to try a deeper sandbox with more sand that would allow this boy to "sink and emerge" through multiple levels of sand and symbol.

It took two months to plan and construct the new deeper sandbox and in that time much healing and growth had transpired for Victor in his weekly appointments. First, the boy who I had taken to calling "the flooder" began adding structure to his creations in the existing box. He entered a "drying out" period where he stopped using water and figures in the box. He would come in and spend a number of minutes just feeling the texture of the sand, running it through his fingers and patting it down, Then working only with sand, he designed a raised amoeba-like creature with a distinct spine that reached to all corners of the creature's body (Figure 8.1). Mirroring the structure that Victor was experimenting with, I began to add structure and boundaries within his sessions. Yes, he could bounce on the exercise ball in the office. No, he could not light the sparkler he found on a shelf. Yes, he could "fight me" with foam-padded "bataka" encounter bats, but we would use the soft, red floppy ones and we would take turns suggesting rules as I reserved veto power for everyone's safety.

Figure 8.1: Victor's Spinal Creature

In the next few sessions, Victor began speaking to me about his fears – fears about what was in his bedroom closet around the time of his father's bout with cancer, and the confusing fears more recently when his brother was driving and drinking with Victor in the car before his removal for treatment. I wondered how Victor could trust anyone after such an experience and decided to test how the trust was between us. As our bataka battles continued, I asked Victor to fight me blindfolded.

Quietly he allowed me to place a red silk scarf over his eyes which had known such fear. Relying only on his hearing and intuition to sense how close or far I might be, he threw himself into the fray and held me off with courage.

I had also started a "hitting contest" (McCarthy 2012, p.149) for young people in my practice who I have taught to pound on a large foam cube with a bataka in order to build up and discharge energy and aggression. For this purpose, I printed and hung a chart above the cube, displaying, for confidentiality, the first initial of the hitter's name next to the number of whacks. After initial "grounding," which I demonstrated to Victor by putting my sock-covered feet one by one on the padded handle end of a tennis racket while taking some weight off the other, I asked him to "choose his weapon." Selecting the solidity and firmness of a heavy Dutch-made bataka, he hit the cube 115 times in his first attempt. He seemed to enjoy this and as he noticed the numbers of "hits" by other contestants growing each week, he would move ahead of the pack at each succeeding session.

I also spoke with Victor about his attention deficit diagnosis, re-defining it as "Attention Possible" as I like to do for my clients diagnosed with ADHD. He smiled briefly at this and moved on to what so many of the young people with attention issues do with equipment they find in my office – work on balance. For Victor this involved vertically balancing a tennis racket with the bottom of its handle on one palm. This soon morphed into a contest, in which he challenged me on who could balance the racket longest. He was pleased with the result. Victor – 55 seconds, Neal – 3. To further support the belief that this young man could recover his balance and build self-confidence, even in the midst of family difficulty, I began asking Victor to "widen his vision" as he worked to maintain balance on a physical and symbolic level. Could his awareness broaden while engaged in "racket practice" to include items on the shelves in the room? Could he slow down enough to take in this wider view while staying on task?

As Victor's evolution, from "liquid to solid" was progressing in and beyond the sandbox he also seemed to be opening to a larger palette of materials and places where his work might take place. He built a boat out of empty plastic bottles, clay, and sticks at one session and launched it into a lake in nearby Central Park to which we had walked. When I spoke to him about my concern that the plastic bottles might end up in the landfill rather than be re-cycled, he emerged at the next session triumphant with a boat tethered to twine that would not float away. While Victor demonstrated increasing ability in session to tether his creativity within a framework of boundaries and rules, reports from his parents about him were also improving. After a session involving the entire family, where we discussed alternatives to what was described by the parents as a "prison" in which evening and weekend time was spent monitoring Victor's schoolwork, he had taken on the responsibility of writing and completing essays for admission to boarding school and had also launched his own snow shoveling business with neighboring boys at his weekend house in rural upstate New York.

Victor welcomed the new deep and waterproof box I had built in response to his "flooding" by taking off his shoes and stepping barefoot into the sand. In the next session, digging deeply and up to his elbows in sand, he excavated a single, yawning canyon in the center of the box surrounded by pile-up on all sides. Into this hole, he placed an empty basketball-sized translucent glass globe, the type used for terrariums. Carefully he nestled the piles around it until the sand was level with the open circular lip of the globe. Now it was time for the water. Walking from the box to the sink, and back again, he slowly filled the globe in silence, moving, almost as if sleepwalking, between source and container bringing clear water to clear glass.

Helping "depth work" to happen with children like Victor was not easy for me at first, especially in the arena of expressive arts that went beyond words. I often felt quite anxious as they created worlds of sand and clay, paper, and ink. Was my role just to watch or could I be more active? To soothe my own restlessness, I had taken on a parallel practice where I wrote my responses in poetry as children expressed themselves through images and structure, reaching for my own inner depth in service of children who were sharing their worlds with me. I did this as Victor's globe filled.

> Water contained in layers of multi-colored sand.
>
> Deep box smoothing the creative urge, magnifying my own clear growth.
>
> Lights dance in crystal round-ness,
>
> My own hands pressing into the mountain.

As the water reached the top of the globe, Victor smoothed the surface of the sand to create a single seamless edge between substances. Each of us smiled, thrilled by the thin glass separating clear, round translucence from sand whose color had deepened to auburn where water had touched it. If asked by a client, I am willing to share my words, but that day Victor did not ask. Silently, he moved to the shelves, selecting a giant purple octopus, my largest sea creature, which he swished and whirled through the currents of water he was generating. This continued for several minutes, his eyes mesmerized and sparkling in the reflected light. Then suddenly, as if a spell has been broken, the boy removed the octopus, plucked four golden fish from the shelves and carefully placed them in the water-filled globe, urging them through the undulating waves of light with his fingers (Figure 8.2).

Figure 8.2: Victor's Globe

Sea creatures rest in the deep waters and emerge

cleansed.

In the silence, my hand

My strong hand

is anointed

in the water

and

breathes.

Victor looked at me with calm deliberation and told me that he would like me to leave this creation for other people to see and make their own additions. I was moved, tears welling up in my eyes. This was my last session with a child before going on vacation and I resolved to leave the box as it was until I returned. I did have one more session scheduled with adults that week – Victor's parents. Dennis had wisely observed in an earlier supervision session, "As this boy changes, either the family will shift… or it will explode." The day after Victor filled his globe, his parents sat in an adjoining room and told me they planned to separate. I felt sadness and grief, glad that I would be leaving for a much-needed vacation.

Nothing could have prepared me for what awaited me a week later when my time away had ended. I looked at the deep box in amazement and shock. The weight of the watery globe had vertically split the seams of the box on two of its sides. It would require repair before the next child could use it as an instrument for self-expression and healing.

Case Study: Kenny, 10 years old

Kenny's father had found my website on the Internet because he was looking for couples counseling for himself and his wife. I generally do such couples work jointly with my wife, Judy Gotlieb, a marriage and family therapist and Core Energetics practitioner like myself, both to provide greater perspective and give us flexibility when family work or separate individual work is required with more than one sibling. This family, like Victor's, had complex presenting symptoms. First and in the forefront of the initial request for couples work, Kenny's stepmother had recently returned from a 30-day stint for substance abuse rehabilitation. The family was looking for therapists who would be sensitive to the role that "recovery" might play in the family's healing. Next, the parents had stepfamily concerns, especially as these related to child-rearing and the children's multi-cultural roots. Kenny's father, a highly successful corporate executive, had first emigrated from Japan to the United States as a college student. He was now divorced from Kenny's mother whose Irish-American forebears had been in the United States for many generations. The stepmother, a Chinese-American woman brought up in the United States, had entered the picture when Kenny was seven, three years after a contentious divorce between Kenny's father and mother.

As matters began to improve two months into the counseling between the father and stepmother, the father requested that I see Kenny because he was fighting with his older sister and refused to help with certain household chores assigned by his parents. Kenny was doing reasonably well in school, a private academy popular with international families. His father knew Kenny was capable of excelling, which he was not.

In walked Kenny to work with me, while his sister arrived to have a session with my wife Judy in a separate office. The first thing I noted with Kenny was that his Caucasian features were so dominant, you would never have known of his Eurasian roots except that he carried his father's Japanese last name, which was emblazoned in big block letters on the baseball warm up jacket he seemed reluctant to take off. Kenny was definitely and firmly "held together" – he looked like a model with well-groomed hair (I later learned that he used gel to keep it in place) and arrived at his first appointment looking like he was ready for a session at an exclusive gym with a personal trainer. Yet there were tears just below the surface and they came out as we talked about how hard it had been for Kenny when his stepmother "yelled" at him, especially while under the influence of alcohol, as Kenny helped her in cooking the family dinner. These meals were eaten very late most weeknights as his father often worked long hours. My sense was that with the exception of disagreements over chores, Kenny was "holding himself together" with his parents. The battles with his sister helped him to release tension from the constant "keeping his emotions under wraps." Kenny's first drawing of himself was an armored monster with tenderness of body and heart held in place by multiple clips that looked like staples, much like the metallic suit of the "Tin Man" from the Wizard of Oz. The face above the metal armoring held eyes askew at different angles and a mouth full of uneven, jagged teeth. Sewn-up scars on the monster's arms hinted at earlier skirmishes and wounds (Figure 8.3, page 152).

Figure 8.3: Kenny's Monster

As the larger deep box had been temporarily de-commissioned after Victor's global waterworks, I brought a deep plastic storage tote into the office to hold the deep sand. Kenny's first sand world inverted the depths of wet sand into discrete towers on which were placed a range of domestic and wild animals. Here, I noticed themes of bigness and wildness (elephant and alligator), and nurturance (swan sheltering eggs, and baby Tiger riding on the back of a turtle), but particularly the separate towers (Figure 8.4). Every figure seemed to have its place, yet each was held aloft – isolated, and alone.

In response, I resolved to facilitate Kenny's emergence from the structures in which he painfully controlled underlying aggression and began what my Core Energetics supervisor Lisa Loustaunau (2014) calls "disorganizing the organized." So I asked Kenny if he would like to have a battle with me in the sand. For this purpose, Kenny selected the larger surface area and shallows of my original box instead of the deeper but smaller plastic tote. There, Kenny prepared his battlements, which included an impressive array of soldiers, a cannon, a small dragon, and a wall-to-wall fence separating his side from mine. Taking a cue from Victor's earlier work in the globe, I selected a giant octopus to battle him and also a large, fire-breathing dragon, which I used to zoom over his fence. Almost immediately, when Kenny's look of dejection and defeat hit me, I knew I'd made a mistake. I offered him a re-match.

This time, he built his defenses deeper into the sand, yet something was not right. It was time again for supervision.

Figure 8.4: Kenny's Separate Towers

The first question from Dennis was, "Had I introduced too formidable a foe? Too much of a salvo?" After all, he counseled, "a dragon can destroy whole villages." As a therapist for a child in pain, I hoped to help "re-organize" this boy into a more sustainable identity within his complex world. Yet how quickly could this, in reality, be expected to occur? Dennis guided me further, "He may not know how to push enough yet." Remarking on the sand pedestals Kenny had created as the elegant opposite of Victor's inverted pool, Dennis prompted me to consider, "Where is his place to stand?" He urged me to try the battle again with Kenny (more on this later) and help him in future sessions to "find solid boundaries" through symbolic means, that he might translate and practically integrate into his family life.

An opportunity for such practical translation happened quickly in the interim. Kenny's father came with him to address his concerns over how his son was disobeying the family rules he had set. One of these linked the regular flow of Kenny's monetary allowance to the chore of taking out the garbage to the incinerator chute down the hall from the family apartment. As I conversed with the boy and his father, what became clear was that Kenny seemed to be enjoying the power he held to refuse and also resented the long hours that his father spent at work. He was especially unhappy waiting for dinner until the father's return each night. As we passed through how all this was operating, I reached for a metaphor that might symbolically take our conversation to a different level, mentioning that under the concrete in Manhattan where our meeting was taking place were the tribal lands of Native Americans now displaced. Seeing that this piqued their interest, I asked Kenny and his father to imagine they were part of such a tribe. How would it function? We discussed the role of his father as the primary "bringer of money" to the tribe and the necessary support roles that Kenny played along with other tribal members. Might the tribe that Kenny was in with his father, stepmother, and sister have a name? Kenny immediately shot back – "the West Side Bun Buns."

Over the next few weeks, I learned that Kenny and his family had sat down at home to meet as the "West Side Bun Buns" and that Kenny had re-negotiated his role from "garbage man" to "dishwasher." Fighting with his sister had become less of an issue. Yet something else was changing in the family system. I knew this soon after the creation of the Bun Bun Tribe, when Kenny carefully drew detailed replicas of the miniature plastic alcohol bottles I have on my sand tray shelves When I called a parent session to learn more about what could have prompted Kenny to draw the bottles, I learned that the stepmother's drinking had indeed re-surfaced. As individual work with Kenny continued, Judy and I referred the stepmother from a couples session to a colleague for individual therapy (at the stepmother's request) and also recommended Alcoholics Anonymous, which she refused as she hoped to be able to drink in a manageable way rather than pursue sobriety with the community support of AA.

Kenny himself was learning to speak up for himself more and more and told his father in a joint session with me that the mother's drinking was not something he wanted to have discussed in West Side Bun Bun meetings. When asked by the father and myself whether this was to be an adults-only issue within the Tribe, he nodded quietly – "Yes." In a subsequent couple's session, both father and stepmother agreed that one of the primary tasks in therapy for Kenny was helping him to remain open with his family in this delicate situation involving adult recovery.

Two boys emerge through family challenge
Close to the time I learned of the relapse of Kenny's stepmother, something was happening with Victor that I didn't know about before. Encouraged by Victor's father to speak with his school psychologist,

I found out that Victor had fainted more than once at school when confronted by teachers about his schoolwork. While the school staff were alarmed, I saw this as a symptom of Victor's emotional flooding at a very confusing time for him. First, his parents still had not told him of their plans for separation, although my guess was that Victor was someone who both sensed and absorbed such family tensions. Second, the months of trying to fit his creative yearnings into the strictures of his school setting were undoubtedly taking a toll. Third, he had no clear indication of where he would be living or going to school after the spring semester was over. Still, I was intrigued. If the fainting was a symptom in response to psychological and emotional flooding, it might actually signal that he was moving forward – albeit in dramatic form. If he could learn to slow down and watch his responses to situations where he felt flooded, perhaps his reactions could change.

Victor had also recently suffered a concussion after slipping on some ice. This, I discovered was not a new or isolated event and provoked additional concern from his parents. There had been more than one concussion in the preceding years – from skateboarding and snowboarding falls. While he had apparently been wearing helmets in these incidents, I knew there was an ongoing battle between the boy and his parents as to whether he would wear protective headgear, with one parent insisting on this and the other often acquiescing to Victor's wish to remain bareheaded. Away from school for several weeks as he healed, Victor's overdue schoolwork was becoming more and more of an issue. In the interim, he had been admitted to a small boarding school that would support his creativity and non-traditional learning styles, but would he complete the academic year, allowing him to move up and out to the new school?

In supervision, I was reminded that as a boy Carl Jung had first suffered a head injury in which he lost consciousness, after which he began repeatedly fainting to avoid going to school and doing schoolwork – and that this feat had been a difficult habit to break. The amazing coincidence about all this was that one of Victor's aunts was a trained Jungian analyst who had told the parents that the challenge with their son would be to "not break his creativity."

What would I do at our next session? Kenny had moved ahead of Victor in the hitting contest – now at 500 whacks on the chart – but I was not about to move into active physical work given the boy's current condition. So Victor and I began discussing, at Dennis' suggestion, the alternatives he might have to fainting when under stress besides thinking of past confrontations with teachers, which further sparked his anxiety. As he draped his body over an exercise ball, Victor had an idea – ironically the same one that the school had come up with when they realized that he could be at risk of hurting himself in a fall when fainting. This time though, Victor seemed to more firmly "own" the idea. "I could sit down," he said.

I thought then of how difficult it had been for Victor's parents to get him to "sit down" to do his schoolwork. I thought of how his parents had been trapped into "sitting down" with him to manage his homework process, and how Victor was learning to sit down on his own to do his work in his own time. Together Victor and I spoke about how his decision to sit down when at risk of fainting was another way he could take care of himself. At one level this was a decision to "ground himself" and to be safe. On a deeper systemic level, we were investigating issues that Victor had struggled with for many years around his need to craft acceptable solutions for himself within a personal and family environment where what appeared as a safe and predictable reality could suddenly shift into danger for him unless he acted with forethought for his own benefit.

After three weeks, Victor received the go-ahead from his doctors to go back to school. It was evident by his renewed level of energy that he was also ready to pick up where he'd left off in his depth work with me. Moving back to the recently returned and repaired deep box, he marveled at the reinforced steel it now sported on all of its seams. I had put slightly less sand in the box this time though, and Victor seemed disappointed that it was not completely full. He asked for the globe and upon receiving it, immediately began pushing its rounded opening into the sand instead of digging a hole in which it might rest like he'd done before. My alarm grew as I realized where this might be heading and I asked him –"Victor, is there another way?" He immediately grunted "No" and resumed his pushing. The globe cracked, a single triangular shard broken out of its frame.

Quickly, I checked his hands for injury and seeing none, he exited the room, shocked and numbed as if sleepwalking towards the adjoining space that held the foam cube and batakas. I too was shocked by what had just happened and remembered what Dennis had said to me in supervision. This boy was having trouble "handling his own intensity" as could be seen in his physical flooding of the sandbox, his emotional flooding as suggested by his fainting, and now the forced cracking of the giant globe. Dennis had said Victor needed help in tolerating his own "big-ness." Could Victor find a way to more fully embody and contain his depths of emotion without "cracking under the strain?" In the next room, Victor was readying his answer.

He had noticed that someone else had surpassed him on the hitting contest chart, and I could see he wanted to start smashing. I stopped him to help him feel and contain his energy for a few moments, reminding him to breathe and first "ground" his feet on a soft tennis ball, before hitting. I could see he was holding his breath. In frustration? In rage? Reluctant to ground, his eyes vacant, he rested each foot for a few moments on the ball and then picked up the heavy, Dutch bataka. As he hit, I observed what looked like fierce, one-pointed dedication to a goal. Straightening his body with his head tilted to the side in concentration, I could sense Victor's deep desire to force the numbers upward – as he later said, "getting a number that no one can beat." I had to remind him to bend his knees to let his entire body flow with the movement. As he finished, flushed, he had hit 550 times, more than doubling his previous record.

Six weeks later, when I saw him at his last session before he left on vacation for the summer, I learned that Victor's parents had told him about their upcoming separation. He had also succeeded in graduating from school. Victor looked bigger and stronger. He also appeared greatly relieved. Now that the separation of Victor's parents and splitting into two households was at the top of the family agenda, Judy and I offered and held a session with the parents alone, focused on cooperation through these next months.

In the meantime, Kenny was preparing to step into more of his authentic self. I told Kenny that I had probably come in too fast with my dragon in our last sand battle and asked him whether he would like help building up his battlements this time. Agreeing, he carefully put figures in the sand world, this time working on both sides. One side contained small, monotone figures in either green army fatigues or blue HAZMAT suits. On the other side, he placed a multi-headed fire-breathing dragon surrounded by trees with its foot resting on a multi-faceted golf-ball-sized diamond. "Who will win?" I asked. "The dragon," answered Kenny. "He will burn them all down." With this, he removed the dragon, placing it on the softness of the corduroy-covered foam cube. Protected under his left claw was the diamond, which sparkled in the light (Figure 8.5). I wanted to know more about the men arrayed on the other side. "They are treasure hunters," he said. I ask him to draw one (Figure 8.6), and as he did, I wrote.

Figure 8.5: Kenny's Dragon-protecting Diamond

Figure 8.6: Kenny's Treasure Hunter

My tenderfoot

Treasure Hunters!
With all your guns and plans…
I, the dragon alone
  in the forest
mouth flaming red,
wings outstretched
  will defeat you.
My tender foot
  resting so lightly
  on the treasure.
I will burn it all.
And I, I am not alone.

I knew that Kenny was holding some very big energy inside. And it began to come out at the next session, which included his stepmother. I had invited her in based on a couple's session where Kenny's father had accused her of "picking on him and Kenny." The stepmother had expressed her frustration that day in "not knowing her place" in the making of rules and carrying out discipline with the children. At this couple's session, the stepmother also told Judy and myself that she had come from a family where her parents "used beating and yelling to teach." After the couple's session, the stepmother had made an apology to Kenny for yelling which she wrote to me about in an e-mail the night before her session with her stepson. "Last night I explained to him the circumstances around my actions towards him. He wiggled and squirmed during my talking but the outcome has been miraculous. He is actively talking to me and his childlike innocence has returned. It is so great that I haven't lost him forever. Now I just have to make sure I don't mess it up."

Noticing the hitting contest on the wall where Victor and others had surpassed him, Kenny hit the cube hard, his stepmother counting. "I feel complete," the boy said, as he fell forward onto the exercise ball to rest for a bit. The family had recently returned from a vacation in the Caribbean and we talked about waves in the ocean, how they crash and fade, much like yelling. I handed Kenny and his stepmother a rope and encouraged them to pull each other in a tug-o-war, the boy surprising his stepmother with his power, the stepmother succeeding in pulling Kenny towards her, ending in a hug.

As we moved to the next room, we pulled the cube with us and Kenny sat on it, drawing a picture of one of his teachers yelling at another boy (Figure 8.7). Kenny cried, remembering when his stepmother yelled at him to turn the lights out in the room because the electricity "costs so much." The stepmother remembered how she too had been yelled at by her parents. I asked Kenny what he could say to his stepmother if it happened again. Kenny said, "I can say 'stop yelling.'" I added, "Can you also say 'it hurts?'"

Figure 8.7: Kenny's Teacher Yells at Another Boy

Over the next few months, there were changes in Kenny's situation. His father took a new job, which kept him busier than before, leaving the boy even more in the care of his stepmother. Couples therapy for his father and stepmother was put on hold. Kenny's constant rotation between his father's West Side Bun Bun apartment in the City and his mother's house in the suburbs led him to create a deep sand tray with a "dream room" at his mother's house where he visited on the weekends. He had to share a room with his sister there but in the "dream room" his sister was "taken out." In the room were jewels he could use to buy anything he wanted including "a helicopter to get me anywhere I want to go" (and perhaps speed the journey between his two homes). Kenny also faced his fury and terror connected with his stepmother's drinking and yelling with greater depth, making a clay model of his stepmother's face and body and then pounding it to a pulp with his fists and a mallet.

Kenny took a month off during his summer vacation, spending it part-time with his father and stepmother as they traveled across the US and part-time with his mother and her husband at their home. When he appeared for his next session, he effortlessly returned to a pattern I see with many active pre-teens, leaping and diving forward onto the large exercise ball again and again, rising and falling, aware of both his body's impact and the sliding, gliding energy of forward momentum. I followed and felt the power of this energy, moving my own head and chin rhythmically forward with each leap, attuning myself to Kenny's movement. Children in families experiencing substance abuse, often feel caught in roiling, unpredictable waves of conflict and change. On the level of mind and emotion they want to distract themselves and escape. Yet they also have a deep longing to test and know the individual power and capability of their own growing bodies. Because I allowed and encouraged the discharge of physical movement in whatever way felt right to Kenny, he experimented and developed a silent, body-centered routine at the start of most sessions, which moved from leaping dives to high and hard bounces, sitting on the big ball. After a minute or two of this, he was up on his feet, jumping twenty to thirty times, gradually adding his shoulders and arms and pumping his fists downward in synchrony with his jumps. I had added this to his routine to energetically harness his "escape" momentum. Children used to regular shocks of displacement in families affected by separation or divorce that have them moving between multiple family systems, go "into their heads," perseverating to block strong feelings of grief, rage, and helplessness or numbing themselves. We were working here beginning with these jumps so that Kenny could literally "feel solid ground" beneath him once again.

Next, I helped Kenny put on punching gloves and invited him to punch a rectangular, padded shield that I held in front of me. I reminded him to be conscious not to "hurt yourself, me, or the room" by avoiding stray punches above or below the shield, or re-coils that would have him knocking things off the walls. Beginning with controlled punches like a prizefighter might use, I asked him to forget the rhythm and "really let go" punching "up from your legs" which he did, surprising me with his power. I thought to myself: is this the same boy who appeared so neatly packaged when he first entered my office six months ago? Finishing his punching, Kenny rested for a minute. He started to collapse and fold forward but I asked him to stand, unlock and soften his knees, taking a position known in Core Energetics as the "bow" posture that "increases grounding and presence"(Loustaunau). The goal here was to complement the "big energy work" he'd just done through an energetic "pulsation" or "vibration" he could feel through his entire body, as the partially exhausted musculature of his legs shook and vibrated gently.

When he first entered my care, Kenny was what we would describe in Core Energetics as "rigidly organized." As my Core supervisor Lisa points out "rigid organization is an attempt to prevent the breakthrough to consciousness of what is experienced as chaotic, dangerous, or unmanageable within." Yet just such a breakthrough is what we look for in the therapy room to free energy and restore fuller self-expression to the client. Thinking that it could be useful to "up the ante" on "disorganizing" Kenny, I handed him a phone book and asked him if he would like to rip it up, which he did with increasing gusto until a good part of the room was filled with paper. I assisted this wildness by adding both rhythmic and random sound from a variety of percussion instruments that included a drum, maracas, a tambourine, and rain-sticks, which created a humorous ceremonial context to the unfolding event.

I initiated the next chapter of madness by picking up a piece of paper and throwing it at Kenny. At first, he threw a few pieces tentatively at me and then as it was clear that we'd be escalating the battle, Kenny picked up a pile and chucked it at me. I responded in kind and we began circling the room like gladiators, throwing larger and larger heaps. He appeared delighted and dropped down in the mess of paper, squirming his body deeper in, as one would revel among gathered leaves in the fall. I covered him up until he was totally buried. He rested for a few moments, and all was quiet. Then suddenly, he emerged forcefully from the heap I demonstrated what it would be like to put paper under my shirt and he made himself fat with paper between his warm up jacket and his t-shirt beneath. He looked proudly at himself, strutting in front of a large mirror on the wall and then ran at me as I held up the blue exercise ball, off of which he bounced. "Hey!" he said, with a big grin, "The paper got flat!" Again, I encouraged him into the "bow" for some standing rest and healing. Finally, he bounced on the ball to end this sequence as first I, and then Kenny, chanted together. "Kenny! Kenny! Kenny!"

After this last session, I asked Kenny's parents to report anything they may have noticed after this particular piece of "big" work. His parents, writing to me by e-mail, described him as "happy and expressive." But with the adults, again all was not well. After a short reprieve, the stepmother was once again drinking. The father said that he had enough and was considering ending the marriage. We recommended that the adults resume the couples work they had taken two months away from, doing this in concert with A.A. and Al-Anon support. They agreed to continue.

Together in session with the West Side Bun Bun adults, Judy and I reminded them that recovery often happens slowly, requiring patience and self-care. No matter what the fate of this second marriage, Kenny would need to grow and negotiate through his complex environment. At the epicenter of four parents, two homes, and a rich variety of multi-cultural roots, you could feel Kenny's hunger to emerge as a unique human being amid the challenges that exist in his life today. The parents wanted me to continue working with Kenny, asking me to see him through whatever is to come.

Epilogue

The writing of this chapter provides a window on therapy with Victor over the course of a year, and Kenny over six months. Shortly before Victor was to leave for boarding school, his parents asked to schedule a session for him a few hours after one scheduled with Kenny.

Kenny, meanwhile

Meanwhile Kenny had been co-creating a story with me in which he, as a young upstart god in Greek mythology, steals the thunderbolts of Zeus and captures the sea from Poseidon. In his session, I asked Kenny if he would re-create his story in the sand tray. Digging a hole in the deep box, he placed a copper colored oval container in the cavity and filled it with water. A dragon guarded the front of the box where he worked protecting his scene along with him. When asked what he wanted to do next Kenny grabbed a small tray of Kinetic Sand, which feels both liquid and solid in the hand. Kneading the sand like dough, he buried first one hand and then the other, breaking out, first one hand and then the other. I was reminded then of Kenny's struggles in the kitchen with his stepmother and how he was learning to resolve them by speaking up for himself.

Victor's arrival

I removed Kenny's creation for Victor's arrival, a patch of darkened sand remained where Kenny's watery oval had been. When Victor walked in, I was struck first by how "together" he looked and how "verbal" he had become, speaking to me proudly about his acceptance as a varsity player on his boarding school's basketball team. Thinking about how much he had learned and had taught me, I gave him a tan manila envelope with something I had drawn up – a "Certificate of Excellence" for "Learning and Self Awareness." Victor smiled, tucking the envelope next to him on the chair.

"Hey, what's that number?" Victor said, looking up at the hitting contest on the wall. "No one beat me in the contest, did they?" I looked. Victor had reached 700 in the hitting contest. "Is that 701?" We both approached the chart. What he didn't know and I couldn't see from afar was that he was looking at the number "201" leading a punching contest Judy had started with other children, which was on the same chart. From far away, the "2" looked like a 7." In the hitting contest, "K" for Kenny was at 650 and Victor was still in the lead, for the moment.

Confidently, he moved to the room holding the sand trays, knowing it would be his last time before school. Fondly pawing and smoothing the sand in the deep box for some minutes, he stood up to check out the tray with Kinetic Sand. For what seemed a very long time, he ran it through his fingers and back into the tray, liquid slipping into solid beneath his hands, smiling with satisfaction. As he spoke of his brother's recovery from alcohol abuse and the prospect of new friends at school, Victor seemed to have a palpably bigger and more mature presence. He seemed more at peace. Whether or not I would ever see this boy again, I knew that he, like Kenny, was emerging with new tools to deal with the challenges of life. And I had been honored to witness two boys in their emergence as young men.

References

Loustaunau, L. (2014) *Charge and Discharge.* Available at www.lisaloustaunau.com/charge-discharge, accessed 28th August 2014.

McCarthy, D. (2012) *A Manual of Dynamic Play Therapy: Helping Things Fall Apart, The Paradox of Play.* London, UK: Jessica Kingsley Publishers.

Pierrakos, J. (1987) *Core Energetics: Developing The Capacity To Love and Heal.* Mendocino, CA: LifeRhythm.

CHAPTER NINE

Musings about Improving and Deepening Connections in Families

Alan Spivack[1]

My life was the size of my life.
Its rooms were room-sized,
its soul was the size of a soul.
In its background, mitochondria hummed,
above it sun, clouds, snow,
the transit of stars and planets.
It rode elevators, bullet trains,
various airplanes, a donkey.
It wore socks, shirts, its own ears and nose.
It ate, it slept, it opened
and closed its hands, its windows.
Others, I know, had lives larger.
Others, I know, had lives shorter.
The depth of lives, too, is different.
There were times my life and I made jokes
together.
There were times we made bread.
Once, I grew moody and distant.
I told my life I would like some time,
I would like to try seeing others.

---

1   Alan Spivack had a major stroke in the autumn of 2013 after beginning
this chapter. He returned to writing it as he was returning to life...
struggling to walk and read and speak.

In a week, my empty suitcase and I returned.
I was hungry, then, and my life,
my life, too, was hungry, we could not keep
our hands off our clothes on our tongues from

Jane Hirshfield

Let me begin with the simple idea that for me deep therapy with children is best exemplified and accomplished when it is possible to include the parents or caretakers of a child. Social worker Mary Jo Barrett, in an article in Psychotherapy Networker Magazine entitled "Outside the Box – Bringing Families into Trauma Treatment" speaks about the deep healing power of a therapist of simply "bearing witness" to the efforts (and failures) at communication within a family (Barrett 2014). Included in my way of working is simultaneously working on attachment issues in the present family, and also with attachment issues for the adults from their families of origin.

I'd like to introduce ideas of child therapy that expand our usual view of children, and which may at the same time deepen this view. For some therapists the deepening process involves that which is primary and fundamental to life, often touching and resolving basic instinctual forces. What I have in mind, however, is the first and foremost instinct – attachment survival. John Bowlby referred to attachment as an instinct. This instinct changes as a child ages, particularly in intensity, but not in depth. The instinct changes with influences from psychological development, temperamental development, biological maturation, genetics, and social influences. All of these influences are there when any therapist encounters a person in their office for the first times. The original attachment instinct is still there, often hidden by that person's life history.

I recently had the opportunity to listen in on a conversation between a newer therapist (I will call him Newbie) and a more seasoned child/family therapist (I will call him Oldster).

Oldster: "I have often wondered how it is that children who have successful therapies come back into therapy with significant problems. Is this just a result of life's twists and turns, and the unexpected difficulties that arise for any organism? Any thoughts about this phenomenon, Newbie?"

Newbie: "I have some thoughts on the subject based on family therapy course work theories I learned. There are structural misalignments in some families where a child is very much allowed into the boundaries of a couple's relationship. Therefore they are dealing with adult issues like money, couple closeness, in-law relationships, and/or other adult relationships. As I remember, with this problem the child takes on false maturity, which alters their authentic developmental growth."

Oldster: "So then you are positing that a play therapist who doesn't sit with the family and child together may not recognize this misalignment pattern? That's a fine theoretical observation, Newbie. You know there are many other family patterns of communication that are extremely complex and can only be recognized by sitting with the child and family and listening very carefully. This listening ideally occurs over a longer time span."

Newbie: "What are you referring to? Do these patterns have names?"

Oldster: "Double Bind Theory, High EE (Expressed Emotion), Projective Identification, Triangulation… I assume from my own therapy practice that interrupting these patterns can make for a deeper therapy – also a more successful therapy for the child's future adolescence and adulthood."

Case Study: Four adolescents

Let me shift gears away from traditional family therapy and look at examples from some cases of mine that are more in keeping with attachment themes.

John Bowlby in *A Secure Base* (1988, p.140) says, "the therapist's role is analogous to that of a mother who provides her child with a secure base from which to explore the world." In one case there were four adolescent children all adopted by their foster family. The family had fostered many other children for over twenty years and seemed to have been very successful parents, as many of those children thrived and kept in contact with them. These four children seemed different – more difficult and intense. The parents were older at this point and some of their resilience for difficulty had eroded. The children each had their own child therapist before the adoption and during it. I began family therapy with the entire family, as that was their preference. The parents were focused on getting improved behavior from each child, that is: better regulation of emotions, more family cohesiveness, and more respectful language.

These children had been severely neglected in their family of origin, by their parents and various uncles and aunts. My therapy was not proceeding well. As the parents demanded better behavior the children's negative behavior seemed to increase. It was obvious that these children had deeper attachment needs that required more attunement to their needs from their parents and myself. The oldest boy, Billy (16 years old), was extremely disassociated from people and his own body. Earlier in his life, when he was first in public care, he'd had a child therapist who had supposedly helped him with these issues. I suggested a meeting with Billy and his new adoptive mother. In the first session I had predetermined to use some techniques from Theraplay, (1988) a family attachment therapy with an excellent evidence-based history of success.

I had spoken to his mother prior to the session about my plans for working on nurturing themes for her and Billy. At one point during the session I sat down on the couch next him. He didn't even seem present in the room. I had noted a series of nasty marks on his arm, as well as disrupted skin from old wounds. When I asked him about the marks he said he had fallen off his bike. I put my hand on his arm and said in my most soothing voice, "That is a bad boo-boo." He hardly acknowledged my touch or language. We spent quite a while with this intervention. I asked him how he felt when the boo-boo happened. I kept touching his arm and saying "that looks like a terrible boo-boo." He showed no emotion or discomfort with either my closeness or my touch.

Before our next session I spoke with his adoptive father about what I had done in the last session and the nurturing I was attempting to give and asked him to attend the upcoming session with Billy. His father had included Billy in many home chores and been very good at teaching him various handyman skills while spending time with him. They seemed to have a strong bond. The father seemed more able to be overtly nurturing with the children and able to be humorous and playful about their misbehaviors. In attachment terms, his behavior repaired the relationships rather than leaving a legacy of hurt and dissatisfaction for all concerned. In the next session I told the father he should come and sit next to his son and use the term "boo-boo" while placing his hands on the marks on the boy's arm. This prompted a response from Billy. He began to spontaneously speak about numerous neglects of his physical body by members of his family of origin. During this span of time in his therapy, Billy became more expressive of emotions and thoughts and his schoolwork markedly improved.

I began to work with the other three children in a similar manner with each parent and child. Jane, also 16 years old, was very secretive, stole things from the family, did not come home many evenings, refused to do any chores, and was verbally insolent.

She would often leave her used sanitary napkins around the house. Unlike her other siblings, Jane did very well in school and had a flair for expressive writing. My early work with Jane was with her alone, attempting to build trust and safety in the relationship. Her mother was worried that Jane was gay as she would only bring girlfriends home. I asked Jane at one point about this worry of her mother's. She laughed heartily and said she loved boys and shared her sexual involvement with several. When I eventually brought her mother into the therapy Jane was very angry with her and it was reported that this was the way they related at home. The mother spoke of Jane's difficult behaviors and I suggested she be more accepting of her and less focused on these behaviors. Once I sensed some warmer feeling between them I asked Jane why she was so angry with her mother. She expressed that she felt only worthwhile as a person when her mother saw "good behavior." She then shared some of her writings and feelings about boys and expressed that she felt wanted and needed in those situations. After much coaching from me, her mother was able to avoid moralizing with Jane. I told her that this honest sharing with Jane could lead to better bonding and more "proper" behavior at home in the future. Jane's attitudes and behaviors improved throughout her senior year of high school and she won a partial scholarship to a fine college. Sadly, she had to leave school in her first year due to peer difficulties and, I suspect, the pressures of being away from home.

Unfortunately, I lost contact with this family as they could not continue therapy. Jane's failure at college could be seen as part of an incomplete therapy as I think she would have benefited from further attachment therapy with her parents. Billy did not finish high school and slowly returned to a very disassociated life. Rather than seeing these as a result of poor family communication patterns, they are examples of the extended amount of time needed and special difficulties involved in helping traumatized children.

Case Study: An eight-year-old boy

I began to see an eight-year-old boy brought to therapy due to extreme bouts of sudden rage at home: threatening people, spitting, biting, hitting, and kicking. Some of these behaviors manifested in school as well. I endured a bloody lip and a black eye in the early weeks of working with this child. Yet he was bright, did well academically and went on to graduate from a military academy. His parents were initially very involved with various behavior modification techniques to improve his behavior. Both parents were professionals and very focused on academic performance. I began to sense that the mother was dissatisfied, frustrated, and seething with anger and the father emotionally disengaged. They reluctantly agreed to my suggestion to come for their own sessions. In my work with them rather than attend to marital issues or differences in parental strategies for their son, I focused on their own attachment histories. The mother had an avoidant attachment history with her own mother and repeated many similar emotional difficulties with her older daughter from a previous marriage. The father had a very unclear memory of his attachment history (with many major gaps of memory), and glossed over difficulties. It also became clear that the parents were focusing on improving the behaviors of the older daughter and losing sight of their son. I gently brought them back to their relationship with their son, Joseph. Eventually I referred them to another therapist for family therapy with their daughter.

When the focus was firmly on the son, we looked at areas of nurture, engagement, structure, and challenge with him and with each of them. As might be expected, the mother needed help in improving her own engagement skills. Father needed improvement with nurture skills as he relied on too much structure for Joseph. As the therapy continued, the mother became more forthcoming and engaged with her son, showing a strong nurturing ability with him. The father was in many ways disassociated from himself and life, but became more able to engage with his son over positive issues, rather than as a disciplinarian.

From my perspective, Joseph improved as his family more positively attuned to his needs for fuller engagement with his whole being. This occurred as his mother and father realized and learned about their own attachment vulnerabilities from their family of origin.

Joseph had been a disregulated child and overtly sensitive from infancy (i.e. very colicky, sleepless, with projectile vomiting, crying at the least upset often for no apparent reason) and these parents were often on edge, feeling they had no more resources to give. They had done the best they could to help Joseph, using suggestions from their families, pediatricians, and other parents. Most of these suggestions were behavioral in nature (such as, let him cry himself out). The parents began to apply methods we had discussed and practiced, many from my practice in Theraplay. Thus the learning for them was not just cognitive, but more active and practical, while testing outcomes in real-time family life situations. Had I seen this family years ago, my focus with them would have been on their own individuation process with their family of origins. The therapy would have used ideas from my training in Bowenian methods (Guerin 1976). There probably would have been no focus on attachment themes. Family therapy has changed. Structural Family Therapy, the most child-focused family therapy, often does not benefit traumatized children or those with neurological problems in my experience. There are now newer therapies that use the lens of attachment issues.

This family attachment effort continued until Joseph was twelve and negotiating school without special classes. His behavior at home improved markedly. He kept up with me by phone until his young adulthood, dealing with issues of intimacy, college and career possibilities, and substance abuse. His parents continued their therapy with me for several years, working with engagement issues such as being more present for each other and nurturing beyond sexual relations. Unfortunately, their life with their daughter did not have a positive outcome.

Some further "musings" about deep therapy are the inclusion of playfulness and humor in the therapy. Rather than formal mechanistic methods meant to foster these two realms, I am referring to a therapist being silly and yet serious with families and taking advantage of spontaneous moments of engendered humor. A family of five: mother, father and three teenage children, came for therapy. They were very anxious about being in therapy and kept focusing on their need for anonymity due to their standing in the community. During one session no one was communicating or talking and we all became very uncomfortable. I was sitting in a very old office chair with wheels and a back that when pushed tended to fall backwards. Out of my own anxiety I had been rocking in this chair without realizing it, until I finally tumbled backwards. Somehow I landed on my feet in a squatting position. We all began explosively laughing and from that moment they began to interact naturally about the serious issues in their family life.

We and our patients co-create our narratives in therapy. As the saying goes "we are all in this together – separately." In the old TV series, *The Lone Ranger*, when they are surrounded by Native Americans getting closer to killing them, the Lone Ranger says to Tonto, "We are almost at our end now." And Tonto replies, "What do you mean 'we'?"

References

Barrett, M. (2014) "Outside the box: Bringing families into trauma treatment." *Psychotherapy Networker Magazine May/June*, available online at: www.psychotherapynetworker.org/magazine/recentissues/2014-mayjun/item/2484-outside-the-box, last accessed 3 February 2015.

Bowlby, J. (1988) *A Secure Base*. Didcot Parkway, UK: Routledge.

Guerin, Jr., P.J., ed. (1976) *Family Therapy – Theory and Practice*. New York, NY: Gardner Press.

Jernberg, A.M. and Booth, P.B. (1998) *Theraplay, Second edition*. San Francisco, CA: Jossey-Bass Publishers.

Hirshfield, J. (2014) "My Life Was The Size of My Life". Forthcoming in *The Beauty*. Newcastle, UK: Bloodaxe Books, 2015. Used by permission of the author.

CHAPTER TEN

A Case for In-depth, Long-term Therapy

Rob Greene

There is an increasing emphasis in the therapeutic world on short-term therapy. This serves the needs of our crowded clinics and insurance companies in whose interest it is to reduce costs whenever possible. Added to this trend is the increasing use of prescription drugs to treat symptoms like depression and anxiety. All of these factors have had the effect of undermining the value of long-term therapy.

Without questioning the helpfulness of short-term therapy or the wise use of psychopharmacology, there is still a strong case to be made for a longer term, in-depth course of therapy. There are three main reasons for this. First, if we recognize that the psyche, like the body, is a self-healing organism we must respect its own inner timing. Second, if the crucial factor in healing is the quality of the relationship between patient and therapist we must allow adequate time for this crucial interaction to develop and resolve itself. Finally, if we view therapy not only as a cure for illness, but rather as an opportunity for personal development and maximizing one's potential, we have to look at the time factor in a whole new light.

So first let us consider therapy as an aid to the self-healing capability of the psyche. In the earliest healing centers in Greece, people came and waited for the God Asclepius to visit them in a dream, hence the word "patient." Thus recognition was given to an inner readiness for the healing process.

Today, dreams provide the trained therapist with vital clues to diagnosis, when defenses are ready to be dismantled, and the nature of the relationship between therapist and patient is revealed. Basically dreams are an attempt of the psyche to correct or balance one's conscious attitude with a compensating point of view from the unconscious. In a dream our inner child may present his school report card to his critical inner parent with fear and trembling, only to discover when it is opened, that he received all "A's." The message clearly is: "You're not as inadequate as you were made to feel growing up. You're actually very intelligent." Or a middle-aged man with an uncontrolled temper dreams of a wolf biting into his heart. This is a clear warning that he is in danger of a heart attack if he does not come to terms with his anger.

First, dreams are often diagnostic. They point not only to anxiety or depression but to the root causes that lie behind the patient's symptoms. Let us take depression as an example. Today it is assumed that depression relates to chemical factors in the brain, often inherited. While this may be true, and the right medication will often relieve the symptoms, I have seldom encountered an instance where depression was not connected to repressed anger or blocked aggression. Within this undifferentiated aggression, often symbolized in dreams as feces, lie a patient's latent initiative and creativity, energy vital to their well-being.

Carl Jung (1984) pointed out that depression is often caused by libido being pulled down into the unconscious to initiate the renewal of the personality. The Book of Jonah in the Bible is the symbolic story of "the Night Sea Journey," namely, how the psychic transformation actually takes place. We are thrown unwittingly into the ocean of the unconscious and swallowed by a whale – depression. There we suffer for the magical three days. But in the whale's belly we carve off and assimilate part of the whale – energy latent in the unconscious. Eventually we are spit out in the East with a renewed energy and a clearer sense of our life's meaning.

Many creative people are familiar with this rhythm, often experiencing depression before a productive period. Those of us who specialize in mid-life changes know this pattern very well. Rather than always treating depression as pathological or a symptom to be removed with medication, it is often wiser to follow it into the depths until we find the treasure hidden underneath. Jung once advised a woman suffering from depression: "When the darkness grows denser, I would penetrate to its very core and ground, and would not rest until amid the pain, a light appeared to me" (Jung *Selected Letters* 1984, p.174).

Sandplay therapy is an excellent example of the psyche's capacity to heal itself, given the proper environment. Here the patient (child or adult) is encouraged to create an imaginative scenario in a sandplay box from a wide choice of figures and objects. No interpretation is made by the therapist. He or she is simply an attentive and caring observer. Gradually by creating a series of scenes over time, people are able to work through inner conflicts on a purely symbolic level. Such a non-verbal approach is especially helpful with children, but even with adults, it gives the unconscious an opportunity to heal us.

All this is to emphasize the importance of observing the natural timing of the psyche in the healing process. No one can predict or prescribe a timetable for the therapy process, as inconvenient as that may seem. The aim of therapy is to harmonize the conscious ego with the unconscious process, not to dictate what should happen when.

The second advantage of a therapeutic process with an unrestricted time frame is the importance of the relationship between the therapist and the client over a considerable period of time. Dr. Irvin Yalom writes: "Research indicates (to no one's surprise) that acute distress can be alleviated quickly, but chronic distress requires far longer therapy, and charactereological changes the longest course of therapy of all." (Yalom 2009, p.224)

A frequently encountered clinical problem is a disconnect in the psyche between the core "Self" of an individual and their conscious ego. Edward Edinger elucidates this clearly in his book *Ego and Archetype*, calling it a break in the "Ego – Self Axis" (Edinger 1991, p.40). Edinger writes:

> A symptom of the damage to this axis is a lack of self acceptance. The individual feels he is not worthy to exist or be himself. Psychotherapy offers such a person an opportunity to experience acceptance. In successful cases this can amount to the repair of the ego-self axis which restores contact with the

inner sources of strength and acceptance, leaving the patient free to love and grow. (Edinger 1991, p.203)

A patient dreamed of visiting a graveyard. He was drawn to a particular headstone and began to dig. He unearthed a small coffin. Inside was a perfectly preserved child still very much alive. This was the core of his childhood "Self" long ago stored away for protection from parents who demanded that he be the child they wanted, not the person he was. In other cases this inner Self has appeared frozen in a refrigerator or stowed in a chest. These examples remind one of Sleeping Beauty the princess put under a spell by a witch, who had to wait, preserved but unconscious, until the right prince came along to kiss her awake.

Creating the safe conditions for this inner child to appear and risk coming into reality is usually a delicate and time-consuming effort requiring a deep level of trust between therapist and patient. More often it is easier to remain unconscious or take a pill to relieve one's symptoms of distress. Yet the long-term benefit for those willing to pursue in-depth therapy is transformation over and against temporary relief.

Long-term therapy honors the fact that the single most important factor in psychological healing is the quality of the relationship between patient and therapist. This personal interaction is the crucial element in healing because most emotional problems have their origin in harmful or dysfunctional family relationships. A child was emotionally abandoned by its parents, or forced to take care of the very adult who was supposed to be caring for him or her, or in an alcoholic household where all feelings were repressed, leaving the child disconnected from his own feelings.

In traditional psychoanalysis the importance of the transference has held a central place. The analyst has been trained to become a projection screen, so the patient's difficulty in relationships will be transferred to the therapist, recognized as projection, and hopefully reclaimed by the patient as his own.

Other schools of therapy, including Jung and Yalom, have emphasized a more interactive, face-to-face exchange between therapist and patient, arguing that if we are modeling real relationships and encouraging self disclosures, it behooves the therapist to be real rather than hidden. Some of the most meaningful interactions in my own therapeutic experiences have come when a therapist admitted their error or shared a relevant personal experience. The constancy of the patient–therapist relationship allows the patient to rebuild his or her trust in a caring other; to relax compulsive self-control and allow dependency to surface; to see his or her own self-worth reflected in the therapist's respect and nonjudgmental attention. This temenos or sacred space cannot be defined in terms of techniques, nor its duration prescribed in the number of sessions required for healing. In fact, the very attempt to do this can be a violation of the healing process.

Finally, it is interesting to note that in the United States we feel that twelve years of schooling plus four years of college are the minimum required to prepare a young person to succeed in life. Most of that time is spent acquiring "outer knowledge." When it comes to "inner knowledge," knowing oneself, a very low premium is placed on this endeavor.

If we looked at therapy, particularly in the formative years, as an indispensible opportunity to expand our consciousness, maximize our creativity, and develop deep and satisfying relationships, what a step toward enlightenment that would be! Instead the general public still views therapy only as cure for illness or an embarrassing necessity when caught in an emotional crisis.

My own practice is mainly one of long-term therapy. And who are my patients? Largely, they are other therapists. They are neither sick nor crippled. By and large, they are highly intelligent, competent professionals who happen to value self-awareness and personal growth. They are committed to wholeness, to being as fully conscious and related as they can be. That was the original meaning of "holiness" – not perfection, but completeness.

If we remove the stigma of illness from psychotherapy and view it as a process of self-actualization, of learning to value the unconscious as an ally in our growth, it becomes a part of our preparation for a fuller life, an opportunity that too few value and take advantage of.

Some individuals, despite having been severely wounded in childhood, have the determination to overcome their handicaps and realize their creative potential. A case in point is a woman who was born into a family with a weak, alcoholic mother and a brilliant but angry bipolar father. She had been in therapy for many years when she came to see me and had achieved an excellent marriage and raised three fine children. However, she was still haunted by fears and could not find the key to her creativity. She had the following dream: "I am in a riding ring and outside in a meadow is a beautiful white horse. He comes trotting toward me but I am afraid, so I lie down by a silver statue for protection. The horse comes closer and nips at me, so I retreat to a nearby house." There she is relieved to find the female housekeeper will be staying for another six months, as she doesn't feel she could manage here alone.

The horse is a common symbol in women's dreams and usually signifies the life instinct. The white horse, however, reminds us of the mythical Pegasus who spring from the body of Medusa when Perseus severed her head. Pegasus represented Perseus's creative energy, now freed from the regressive pull of the unconscious symbolized by Medusa's power to paralyze her victims.

When an animal bites one in a dream, instinctive energy is trying to engage with the dreamer. Her attitude toward the creature is crucial. Will the dreamer engage with the energy or run away?

In this case the dreamer retreats, first seeking the protection of the silver statue. Silver is the "moon metal" and the moon with its monthly phases of course is a feminine symbol. The dreamer is trying to be protected by the feminine. She then seeks the further protection of the house and housekeeper, still remaining in the shelter of the feminine. She is still frightened by the power of her masculine creative potential contaminated by a harsh angry father.

In active imagination the patient agreed to go inside and reengage with the horse. She stroked its neck and eventually summoned the courage to get on and ride it. The dreamer, now in her fifties, is gradually claiming her own creative power as a writer, but it has taken her years of hard work in several venues of therapy to defeat her demons and claim what is hers.

If one engages in the challenge of individuation, of claiming one's own wholeness, there is no shortcut. One may engage in therapy off and on for many years, circumambulating the same complexes over and over but at deeper and deeper levels. The rewards, however, are not limited to our own personal well-being. The effect of increased consciousness and the capacity to relate more caringly and fully to others is passed on not only to our children and loved ones, it adds something indefinable but invaluable to the world at large. As the Gnostics imaged it, in therapy we are gathering the scattered fragments of our personal light together so our small light may be added to that of others and increase the level of consciousness, responsibility, empathy, and compassion in a world so desperately in need.

References

Edinger, E. F. (1991) *Ego and Archetype: Individuation and the Religious Function of the Psyche.* Boston, MA and London, UK: Shambhala Publications.

Jung, C. (1984) *Selected Letters,* 1908–1961. Ed. Gerhard Adler. Princeton, NJ: Boingen Press.

Yalom, I. (2009) *The Gift of Therapy: An Open Letter to a New Generation of Therapists and their Patients.* London, UK: Harper Perennial.

Epilogue

Dennis McCarthy

"Love is the deepest knowledge of things. We can reach reality only through love" (Nishida 1990). While editing this book I witnessed and participated in hundreds of children's sand world creations and listened to the dreams of numerous adult patients. The innate desire to speak about our lives through images, and to attempt to connect with "the other" and to ourselves through this connection, is always a revelation. Even when we fail in these efforts, the impulse to do so is moving. The struggle to become upright, to regulate our own intensity without putting the fire out or burning ourselves and others is deeply moving, even if it may cause great pain at times. If we see, feel, hear, and sense with Nishida's comment on love kept in mind, then the way forward is possible. The reality of love may seem naïve when faced with enormous pain. What good is this knowledge in a war torn, violent world? But love can in fact show us the way forward through the labyrinth. Then the heartaches we hear about and the wounds we see revealed in play may become intertwined with moments of joy that arise from the creative process. The deeply wounded child sits by the sandbox and makes a world in which the forces of evil battle with the forces of good. Beneath it all lies a powerful treasure, named alternately "the spark of life" or "the goblet of light that dispels darkness" or simply "the one." It is this capacity that can make an impasse a portal, a seemingly hopeless situation have potential. In the shadow of an unraveling world, it offers some glimmer of hope for each of us and for all of us.

For The Children

The rising hills, the slopes,
of statistics
lie before us.
the steep climb
of everything, going up,
up, as we all
go down.

In the next century
or the one beyond that,
they say,
are valleys, pastures,
we can meet there in peace
if we make it.

To climb these coming crests
One word to you, to
To you and your children:

Stay together
learn the flowers
go light.

Gary Snyder
(with permission from Gary Snyder,
Turtle Island, New Directions, 1974, NY)

References

Kitaro, N. (1990) *An Inquiry into the Good*. New Haven, CT: Yale University Press,
    p.174.

Contributors

Dr. Sue Jennings, PhD, is a traveller and playful pioneer of Neuro-Dramatic-Play and Embodiment-Projection-Role, which are taught worldwide on play and dramatherapy courses; she is Visiting Fellow Leeds Beckett University and Visiting Professor Taiwan National University of the Arts; she has authored some 47 books on various topics connected with play and drama. Her doctoral fieldwork happened in the Malaysian rainforest where she lived with her three children. More information can be found at www.suejennings.com, www.playanddramapartnership.org, and www.creativecareinternational.org. Contact: drsuejennings@hotmail.com.

Timothy Rodier, LCSW-R, is a psychotherapist in private practice in Kingston, NY working with children, adolescents, and adults. For a decade, he worked as a clinician and supervisor in community mental health providing individual and group therapy for adults with severe and persistent mental illnesses. Tim uses his years of training in psychodynamic psychotherapy, as well as dynamic play therapy and sandplay, to help adults, children, and adolescents better understand and relate to the unconscious processes that guide their emotions, behaviors, and relationships.

Julie Lyon Rose, HMC, began dancing 56 years ago and danced professionally with Kei Takei's Moving Earth Company, among others, in the 1970s and 80s. She performed and recorded with composer Pauline Oliveros, as a dancer and vocalist, for ten years and presented her own site-specific dance events in California and the Hudson Valley, as co-founder of Cormorant Dance Foundation. She has taught all ages and many forms of movement since 1973. She has practiced T'ai Chi since 1972 and has a second-degree black belt in Tang Soo Do. She practices body-centered psychotherapy, play therapy and homeopathic medicine in Accord, NY.

Michelle Rhodes, LCSW-R, ATR-BC, NCPsyA. Michelle Rhodes has a private psychotherapy practice in Gardiner, NY and in New York City. She is also a clay artist and maintains a clay studio in Gardiner, which is connected to the therapy space and playroom, providing an opportunity for active and messy expressive work. She holds graduate degrees from Lesley University (expressive therapy) and Adelphi University (clinical social work) and has completed psychoanalytic training at the Institute for Expressive Analysis. She works with all ages, encouraging the use of sandplay, art therapy, and intermodal expressive therapy to facilitate healing and personal growth.

Tim Woodhouse is a registered non-directive play and filial therapist, EMDR practitioner, sensorimotor psychotherapist and ABE-approved social worker who has worked therapeutically with children since 1991. He was a tutor on the Liverpool Hope MA and PG Dip course in play therapy and a visiting lecturer to Manchester University's Second Year MA social work programme. He worked for the UK national children's charity NSPCC for 15 years and was a founding member of St. Mary's SARC children's sexual assault referral centre in Manchester. He is the founder and director of Tiptoes Child Therapy Service – a provision that provides assessment and therapeutic services for children affected by sexual trauma, for children who have sexually harmed others, and children with disrupted and insecure or disorganized attachment patterns.

Therese Bimka, MA, LCSW, is passionate about the interface between psychological work and spiritual growth. Bringing deep wisdom and skillful engagement to the work of healing and transformation, Therese works with children and adults incorporating a diverse range of modalities including Jungian Sandplay Therapy, expressive arts, SoulCollage®, guided visualization, dreamwork, and a host of mind/body spirit practices which she incorporates into work as a psychotherapist in private practice and as a workshop leader and teacher. Clinically trained since 1995, Therese has a special interest in attachment, trauma, and in finding authentic meaning, purpose, and passion despite the challenges we may face externally or internally. In addition to her private work, Therese completed her seminary training as an interfaith minister and is the director of The One Spirit Interspirtual Counseling Program where she designs curriculum and trains interfaith ministers and wellness practitioners nationally and internationally in the art of spiritual counseling, which entails clarifying and deepening a personal and intimate relationship with the divine in whatever form that may take.

Dennis McCarthy, LMHC, trained initially as a dancer and dance therapist and went on to train in Bioenergetic Analysis and Jungian Analysis, and was in treatment in all three modalities. With 40 years of experience, he created his own approach to play therapy that is body-centered and imagination-driven. He has authored many articles and several books on his work. He trains and supervises many therapists and maintains a large private practice in Kingston, NY. He also leads a biannual workshop for personal growth in the Greek islands called "The Heart Leaps Up..." that explores the overlap of personal process and mythic story.

Neal Brodsky is the co-creator of Core 4 Kids (Core Energetics for Kids) and a holistic psychotherapist who uses expressive therapies to help both young people and adults create lives they love. He is licensed in Marriage and Family Therapy. Neal is the author of poetry on the topic of divorce as well as the articles "Finding The Lost Boys: A Therapist Talks About Teens" and "Finding The Sweet Spot In A Second Marriage," each published in the November 2012 edition of the East Coast Sandplay Journal. More information on Neal's work can be found at www.nealbrodsky.com and www.core4kids.com.

Alan Spivack, LCSW, has practiced family therapy for over 30 years with all age groups. His postgraduate training was at The Family Institute of Westchester, where he studied with Norman Ackerman, Betty Carter, and Monica McGoldrick. Prior to private practice he was director of the first forensic team in New York state associated with the family court system. He was also trained in Theraplay.

Richmond Greene is a Licensed Psychotherapist and Jungian Psychoanalyst, and former President of the C.G. Jung Institute of New York. He leads ongoing dream groups for therapists. He is also an accomplished painter.

Subject Index

abuse
    emotional 86, 93
    physical 83, 86
    sexual 129
    substance abuse 64, 72, 75, 86, 130,
        144–5, 150–1, 154, 161–2, 164,
        176–7
abuse dichotomy 93, 96
Active Imagination 49, 178
adoption 144–5, 167–8
    see also foster care
aggression 67–8, 84, 126–9, 132, 135–7,
    140, 147, 152, 170
    suppressed/blocked 19–20, 127, 136,
        174
alcoholism see abuse, substance abuse
anger/rage 39, 47–8, 50, 76, 84, 86–7,
    170, 174
anorexia 133–4
anxiety 19–20, 46, 83–4, 86, 89–90, 97,
    126, 132, 135, 156, 173–4
    separation 54, 57
    social 72
archetypes 18, 50, 73–4, 100–5, 110,
    115, 124–5, 175
Asperger's Syndrome 38, 60
attachment 23, 30, 33, 68, 81, 83, 96,
    101, 114, 166–71
    attachment therapy 169
attention deficit disorders 39, 144, 147

bioenergetic see therapy, bioenergetic
bipolar disorder 178
Buddhism 102, 104, 121, 126

castles 89–90, 137
caves 38–42, 49–50, 56, 67, 69, 76, 96,
    134, 138
chaos 55, 65, 67–9, 72, 74–5, 77, 84,
    89–90, 101, 137

child birth 30–3, 34, 48, 108
clay 12, 19, 39, 56–7, 60, 66–7, 71, 125,
    128, 130–1, 137, 147–8, 160
Core Energetics see therapy, Core Energetics

death 15, 29, 32, 41–2, 62, 64, 74, 76,
    78, 94, 97, 108
depression 86, 126, 173–5
digging
    psychologically 10, 39, 50, 94, 96, 127,
        176
    in sandplay 39, 44, 54–7, 62–3, 65, 75,
        91, 94, 125, 139, 148, 156, 163
dissociation 81–2, 88, 129, 168–170
divorce/separation 127, 133, 150, 157,
    161
Double Bind Theory 167
dragons 10, 76, 121, 136, 140
    in clay 66–8, 75
    in dreams 121
    in sandplay 44, 47, 56, 138–9, 152–3,
        157–9, 163
dreams 27, 29, 33–4, 49, 53–4, 57, 73,
    121, 160, 173–4, 176, 178, 181
drugs
    prescription 144, 173–4
    see also abuse, substance abuse
dyspraxia 88, 91
dyslexia 136

echolalia 19–20
Embodiment-Projection-Role 30
embodiment 30–1, 54, 57, 103, 110, 113,
    135
epiphany 53
expressive arts 100, 143, 148

fear 27–8, 39, 58, 60, 72, 84, 86–7, 90–1,
    93, 95–6, 121, 130–1, 146–7
    confrontation of 41, 147, 178

floods 71, 77, 131, 144–5
    emotional 132, 145, 155–6
    in sandplay 60, 65, 67, 69, 71, 130–1,
        144–6, 148
foster care 81, 83, 85, 91–2, 167
    see also adoption
Freud, Sigmund 73

gems 62, 68–70, 77, 128, 132
    see also treasure
goddesses 106
    fertility 70, 77
    Isis 48
    mother 44, 46, 50
    snake 61, 69, 71, 73, 78, 108
    Vinita 108
grounding 123, 126, 130, 135–6, 138,
    147, 156–7, 161

healing séance see séance
hibernation 106, 108–9
High Expressed Emotion 167
horses 69, 77, 128, 178
    Pegasus 178

Indra 102–3

Jung, Carl 42, 49, 73, 100, 102–4, 114,
    155, 176, 184

Kundalini 106

loneliness 48, 54, 82–4, 91, 115–6, 152

monsters 43–6, 63, 71, 73, 96, 121,
    130–3, 137, 151–2
mythology 33, 38, 41, 102, 105–6, 133,
    145, 163

neglect 83, 86, 92, 104, 168–9
Neuro-Dramatic Play, NDP see play, neuro-
    dramatic

obsessive compulsive disorder 72, 75

phallic 27, 65, 75, 78, 133
phobias 60, 72–3, 132
Plato 136
play
    aggressive 132, 137
    cathartic 128, 130–1
    deconstructive 123

deep 23–5, 27–8, 31, 33–4, 99, 106,
    112, 117–8, 122–3, 125
    imaginative 50, 110, 121, 133, 175
    Neuro-Dramatic 25, 30–1, 33
    repetitive 131
    risky 24
    rhythmic 33
    sensory 31–3
    symbolic 115, 124, 175
    unstructured 101
play therapy 30, 66, 72, 88, 122, 124–6,
    136
    dynamic 39, 48
    Jungian sandplay 100, 102, 105, 110,
        114–5
poetry 53–4, 57, 105, 143, 148
portal 38–9
power 37–8, 41, 47–8, 68, 70, 77–8, 101,
    104–5, 109, 114, 116, 128, 133,
    145, 161, 178
prescription drugs see drugs, prescription
Projective Identification 167
psyche 69, 74, 92, 100–6, 113, 122, 124,
    136, 173–5
psychoanalysis see therapy, psychoanalysis
psychopharmocology see drugs, prescription

regression 45, 54, 96–5, 125, 131–2,
    134–5
repression 19, 39, 95–6, 123, 176
resourcing 89–90
reverie 64, 73–5
revolution 53–4, 56–7, 140

safety 54, 82–3, 90–1, 94, 97, 99, 106,
    115, 169
Saint Francis 42
sand 38–9, 43–4, 46–7
    deep 53–4, 91, 113, 125, 131, 134,
        152, 160
    dry 39, 70, 146
    wet 57, 60–5, 67–70, 91, 152
    quicksand 44, 77
séances 26–30, 32, 34
self 50, 53–4, 99, 101–4, 107, 109–10,
    113–5, 117, 122, 128–9, 175–6
    self-actualization 100, 177
    self-assertion 124, 128, 132, 138
    self-awareness 124, 164, 177
    self-confidence 147
    self-consciousness 136

self-control 177
self-esteem 47, 110
self-expression 128, 140, 150, 162
self-healing 173
Senoi Temiars 24–8, 30–4
sensory processing disorder 46
separation anxiety see anxiety, separation
sexual abuse see abuse, sexual
sexuality 49, 86, 90, 96, 123–4, 137, 140, 169, 171
shamans 26–30, 32, 49
shame 85, 96
snake goddess see goddesses, snake
snakes 55, 67–9, 71, 77–8, 88, 96, 106–8
social anxiety disorder see anxiety, social
soul 29–30, 99, 104–6, 110–2
  blood-soul 32
  head-soul 26, 29, 32
Soulcollage® 100, 102–3, 105
Structural Family Therapy see therapy, Structural Family Therapy
substance abuse see abuse, substance abuse
swamps 63, 65, 67–9
  see also water
syzygy 67

Theraplay see therapy, Theraplay
therapy
  bioenergetic 124
  Core Energetics 143, 150, 152, 161–2
  long-term 175–7
  see also play therapy, dynamic,
  see also play therapy, Jungian sandplay
  psychoanalysis 42, 176
  see also Soulcollage®
  Structural Family Therapy 171
  Theraplay 168, 171
tics 96
tigers 25–9, 32–3, 133, 152
trance 26–7, 29–30, 33, 84
treasure 62, 65, 68, 70–1, 76–7, 97, 109, 131, 134, 139, 157, 175, 181
  see also gems
Triangulation 167
tunnels 37–48, 50–1, 96–7, 112–3

unconscious 39, 48–50, 114–5, 174–5, 177–8
underworld 106, 122–3

violence 27, 39, 69, 83–7, 90

water 57, 60–4, 67–9, 71, 113–5, 130–1, 144–6, 148–50, 152, 163

Author Index

Amatruda, K. 114
Andrews, T. 106
Archer, C. 82

Barrett, M.J. 166
Batmanghelidjh, C. 85
Benjamin, G. 26, 32–3
Bowlby, J. 166, 168
Brach, T. 104
Briere, J. 93
Brown, F. 24
Brown, F. 24

Cairns, K. 84–5
Ciccheti, D. 81
Cozolino, L. 23, 31, 83

Damasio, A. 125–6
Dietz, R.S. 93

Edinger, E.F. 175–6
Erikson, E. 131, 136
Estes, C.P. 87

Frost, S. 102–3
Fuller, L.L. 24

Garite, T.J. 86
Geertz, C. 24–7
Gordon, C. 82
Guerin, Jr., P.J. 171

Herman, J.L. 83
Howe, D. 81
Huxley, L. 140

Iacoboni, M. 82

Jennings, S. 25–6, 31, 33
Johnson, R.A. 49
Jung, C. 101, 174–5

King, S. 82
Kitaro, N. 181
Klin, A. 60
Kurtz, R. 84, 90

Levy, T.M. 93
Loustaunau, L. 152, 161
Lowen, A. 123–4, 126

Macfie, J. 81
McCarthy, D. 30, 147
McPartland, J.C. 60
Minton, K. 84–5, 88, 91

Neumann, E. 42–3

Ogden, P. 84–5, 88, 91
Orlans, M. 93

Pain, C. 84–5, 88, 91
Palmer, P. 99, 111
Patte, M. 24
Piccard, J. 93

Reich, W. 123–4

Salman, S. 134
Sandman, C.A. 86
Shakespeare, W. 23
Sharp, D. 103
Siegel, D. 82, 84, 90, 101, 117
Simpson, P.H. 114
Sobel, D. 42
Some, M.P. 101
Sutton-Smith, B. 24

Toth, S. 81

Ulanov, A. 126

Volkmar, F.R. 60

Wadhwa, P.D. 86
Welwood, J, 104
Whyte, D. 121
Winnicott, D.W. 50

Yalom, I. 175